Milk Street is changing how we cook by searching
the world for bold, simple recipes. Adapted
and tested for home cooks everywhere, this is what
we call the *new* home cooking.

CHRISTOPHER KIMBALL'S

MILK STREET

C H R I S T O P H E R   K I M B A L L

THE COMPLETE
MILK STREET
TV SHOW COOKBOOK

2017–2019
Every Recipe from Every Episode of the Popular TV Show

Christopher Kimball

J.M. Hirsch, Matthew Card, Michelle Locke,

Jennifer Baldino Cox and the

editors and cooks of Milk Street

LITTLE, BROWN AND COMPANY

NEW YORK   BOSTON   LONDON

Little, Brown and Company
Hachette Book Group
1290 Avenue of the Americas, New York, NY 10104
littlebrown.com

Revised and Expanded Edition: October 2018

Little, Brown and Company is a division of Hachette Book Group, Inc. The Little, Brown name and logo are trademarks of Hachette Book Group, Inc.

The publisher is not responsible for websites (or their content) that are not owned by the publisher.

The Hachette Speakers Bureau provides a wide range of authors for speaking events. To find out more, go to hachettespeakersbureau.com or call (866) 376-6591.

Photography Credits: Connie Miller of CB Creatives. Other photography by page: Channing Johnson, pages VI-VII, 410-411; Joyelle West, pages: 119, 217, 272; Shannon Frandsen, pages XI, XVIII-XIX; Michael Piazza, pages 54, 108, 309, 328; Kristin Teig, pages: 22, 24-25, 221; Heidi Murphy of White Loft Studios, page 80; Sylvain Cherkaoui, pages XII-XIII; Marco Simola, pages XIV-XV; Noam Moskowitz, pages XX-XXI.

Styling Credits: Christine Tobin except as noted: Catrine Kelty, pages 22, 24, 25, 27, 54, 72-75, 80, 87, 103, 108, 111, 134, 143, 221, 226, 231, 250, 307, 309, 321-322, 327-328, 330, 333; Catherine Smart, pages 116, 122-123, 127, 146, 238-239; Monica Mariano, pages 248, 336; Brianna Coleman, page 122; Molly Shuster, pages 29, 84, 90, 165, 192, 237, 347; Sally Staub, page 300.

ISBN 978-0-316-41584-2
LCCN 2018943003

10 9 8 7 6 5 4 3 2 1

IM

Print book interior design by Gary Tooth / Empire Design Studio
Printed in China

This book is dedicated to the
notion that cooking is the universal language
of the human spirit.

Contents

THE NEW HOME COOKING

The Marché Tilène, or Tilene Market, in Dakar, Senegal, is a vast airplane hangar of a place, with light filtering down through the open roof. I walked past long stretches of wooden benches covered with fish, from sardines and the popular thiof (similar to sea bass) to grouper, prawns and large barracuda, one specimen reaching 7 feet. We found a good spot to introduce our episode on the cooking of Senegal, then I did two takes (cameras are not welcome in Dakar, so we did not linger). Then we bought mangoes, oranges, a couple of cheap blue plastic grocery sacks and an assortment of Maggi seasoning cubes on the way out.

The previous afternoon, we cooked the local seafood gumbo and then, after our market visit, we spent the day with Pierre Thiam, a Dakar-born New York chef who prepared a sweet potato/black eyed pea stew, a mango-avocado salad and rice pudding with coconut milk. We also stopped by a cavernous "dibi" restaurant, where thin slices of beef, liver and chicken are cooked over table braziers, the guests seated around, paying for whatever they eat. The meat is served on used green-lined computer paper along with mustard, hot sauce, grilled onions and powdered spices. Hold the skewer at one end, dip the cooked meat in the condiments, slide the seasoned meat into your mouth.

This book is about that trip and others like it, including Cape Town, Taipei, Armenia, Peru, Columbia, Thailand, Italy, Mexico and dozens of other destinations. We travel the world to spend time with cooks who help us appreciate new ways of thinking about cooking, flavor and the art of eating. Our journeys leave us feeling both humble (how did we live so long without harissa?) and thrilled to discover that the development of flavor in cooking does not have to be a function of time and expertise. It's actually rather simple—start with big flavors and the cooking takes care of itself. With liberal use of spices, herbs, chilies and fermented sauces, anyone can become a good cook virtually overnight.

In this volume, you will find all of the recipes from the first two seasons of Milk Street Television. These are not authentic reproductions of the recipes we enjoyed elsewhere; these are adaptations of those recipes for the American kitchen. We don't call for ingredients you won't find in the supermarket (no smoked catfish in the gumbo, for example) or techniques that make no sense in our homes (no pounding of okra in a 3-foot-high wooden mortar and pestle). We have limited time in the kitchen, as do you, and our batterie-de-cuisine is a bit different than Dakar or Chiang Mai.

But the kitchens we visited in Dakar are not all that different than what you might find in Europe or America. The world is growing smaller and it is time to reach out across the oceans and continents to find better ways to put food on the table. Nothing fancy. No feasts; only suppers. But the world has a lot to teach us about flavor, about combinations of ingredients, even about how to cook an egg.

I hope that you enjoy the television show, as well as this book. Milk Street was founded to change the way we cook. It has already changed mine.

Christopher Kimball
Founder, Christopher Kimball's Milk Street

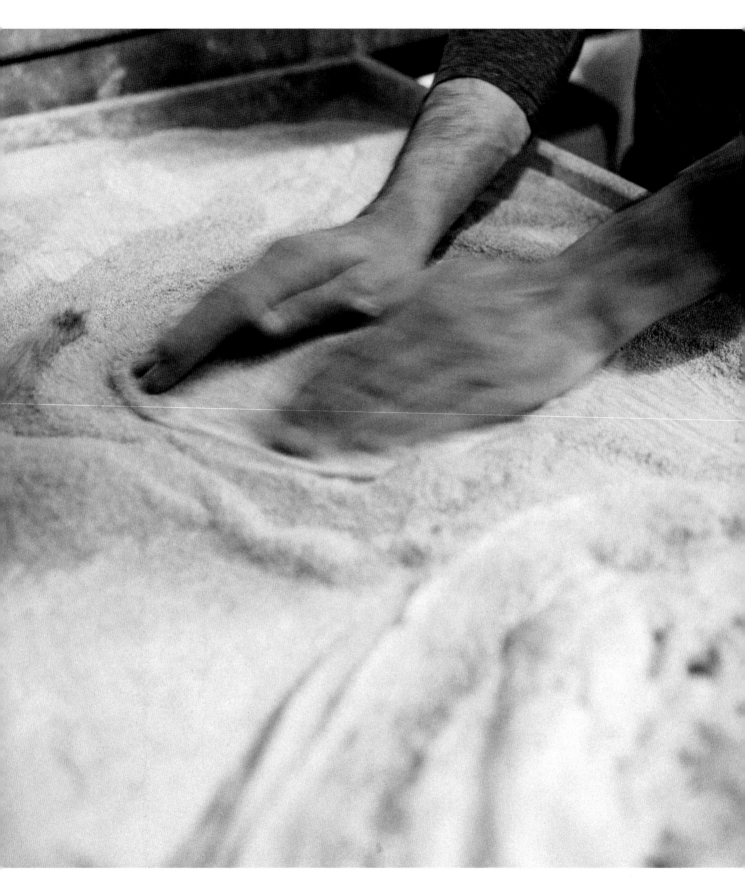

Pantry

1

PANTRY

FATS

Butter

Breaking with convention, we use salted butter for everything. Our reason? It simply tastes better. Not to mention it's simpler to keep just one variety of butter on hand for all uses, whether for toast or cooking. Our recipes are written with the extra salt of salted butter in mind (roughly ¼ teaspoon per 4-ounce stick). To use salted butter in other recipes that assume unsalted, scale back slightly on other salt added during cooking. If using unsalted butter in Milk Street recipes, add a pinch more salt than specified. Butter readily absorbs surrounding flavors, so store it tightly wrapped in the refrigerator. For longer storage, it can be frozen.

Coconut Oil

Coconut oil is a fat we use sparingly, generally with other coconut ingredients. Its flavor is particularly good in Indian and Southeast Asian dishes. Be mindful of its low smoke point.

Cooking Spray

We use nonstick cooking spray judiciously. It's convenient and works well (the lecithin in it ensures that even the stickiest foods release). Baking spray, which contains flour, is ideal for coating baking pans, especially a Bundt pan's deep grooves.

Grapeseed Oil

We like the neutral flavor, light mouthfeel and high smoke point of grapeseed oil. It's our go-to choice for a neutral cooking oil.

Lard

Though it's a four-letter word for many, we think lard has a place in modern cooking. It tastes awfully good stirred into a pot of beans or used to add flakiness to savory baked goods. Most supermarkets sell Armour brand lard, which is hydrogenated (in some stores, it will be easier to find Armour labeled in Spanish as "manteca"). Lately, high-quality lard has become more widely available; look for it in jars. If you can find it, "leaf" lard has the lightest flavor. Lard keeps indefinitely in the refrigerator or freezer but will absorb other flavors; wrap it well.

Olive Oil

We probably use olive oil more than any other oil. In most cases, we favor full-flavored extra-virgin olive oil. Buying extra-virgin olive oil is a gamble; expense doesn't always guarantee quality, and there are few safeguards against adulterated oils. While there are wonderful imported oils, we think California oils are generally fresher and a better bet. California Olive Ranch extra-virgin olive oil, for example, is a terrific product that can be found in most any supermarket. Regular olive oil—not extra-virgin—is made from subsequent pressings and thus lacks the more robust flavor of extra-virgin. Its mild flavor and higher smoke point make it better for sautéing.

Peanut Oil

The light, nutty flavor and high smoke point of peanut oil make it particularly good for deep-frying. Toasted peanut oil has a more pronounced nutty flavor.

Sesame Oil

Sesame oil is pressed from either raw or toasted seeds; we prefer the richer flavor of the latter, which we drizzle over many Asian dishes. As with most seed and nut oils, sesame oil is volatile and can go rancid. We recommend buying small bottles that can be used within a couple of months. Sesame oil has a low smoke point and is not suitable for sautéing.

Tahini

Tahini is a paste made from ground sesame seeds. Good tahini is pleasantly bitter. As with sesame oil, it can be made from raw or toasted sesame seeds. We often prefer the stronger flavor of the latter and, when possible, stone-ground varieties (the label should indicate). Tahini is fine for a month or less at room temperature, though we recommend refrigeration beyond that to maintain freshness. Try stirring it into yogurt with a little jam, smearing it on toast with honey or drizzling it over roasted chicken or vegetables.

ACIDS

Cider Vinegar

The mildly acidic, lightly fruity flavor of cider vinegar is neutral enough to work in numerous dishes, making it a vinegar we turn to often. The flavor varies by brand; we prefer Bragg Organic Raw Unfiltered Apple Cider Vinegar.

Citrus

The zest and juice of lemons, limes and oranges show up repeatedly in our cooking. They are excellent for balancing the flavors of other ingredients, especially anything heavy or fatty. A spritz of lemon or lime juice before serving can brighten most any finished dish. When shopping for lemons and limes, look for round, plump fruit that feel heavy for their size. They should also give when squeezed; hard fruit won't produce much juice. Citrus should be stored in the crisper drawer of your refrigerator to maintain freshness. Use a wand-style grater for zesting citrus. It produces light, feathery shreds that blend easily into dishes. Make sure to avoid the white pith beneath the zest, which can be bitter. If you need the zest but not the juice of citrus, be sure to wrap the fruit in plastic or a bag, otherwise it will dry out quickly. There are countless ways to juice citrus fruits (juicer, reamer, fork, tong tips), though we do recommend squeezing it over a small mesh strainer to catch seeds. For recipes calling for both zest and juice, it's easier to zest before juicing.

Pomegranate Molasses

Intensely sweet and sour, pomegranate molasses is used throughout the Middle East in both sweet and savory dishes. It's essentially boiled-down pomegranate juice that is rounded out with a bit of sugar and acid. We like it drizzled over grilled or roasted meats or vegetables just before serving, mixed with Greek-style yogurt for a simple dip, or added to vinaigrettes. It pairs particularly well with Aleppo pepper. Refrigerated, an open bottle will last indefinitely, though it may need to be warmed in hot water or the microwave before it will flow freely.

Sherry Vinegar

Used liberally in Spanish and French cooking, sherry vinegar has a complex, slightly nutty flavor. The best sherry vinegars have a little age on them, which softens the harsh edges. Look for labels indicating the vinegar is at least 3 years old. It will cost a little more than unaged vinegar, but the difference in flavor is worth it.

Unseasoned Rice Vinegar

Rice vinegar is a staple of Japanese cooking and packs a mild, neutral acidity well suited to vegetables, seafood and poultry. It can also add kick to citrus juice. Be sure to purchase unseasoned rice vinegar; seasoned rice vinegar is used for making sushi rice and already contains salt and sugar, which can make it difficult to balance in dressings.

Verjus

Verjus is the cooking wine substitute you've been searching for. While fruit juices or vinegar can work, verjus—made from the juice of unripe wine grapes—adds a gentle mineral tang and a wine-like body. Verjus can be tricky to find and may require purchasing online. Refrigerate after opening to prevent spoilage. It will last for two to three months.

White Balsamic Vinegar

White balsamic has little to do with the dark, sweet, long-aged stuff most people are familiar with. But its light, neutral flavor and mild sweetness make it an acid we use often. White balsamic is perfect for when we want a clean flavor that highlights, but doesn't compete with, other flavors.

FRESH HERBS

We use fresh herbs with reckless abandon to add bold, bright flavor to many of our recipes. Instead of scant tablespoons, think in terms of handfuls. It's important to wash and dry herbs well. Any moisture clinging to them can turn them mushy during chopping and dilute the flavors of the dishes to which they are added. Salad spinners work best. Herbs can also be dried by rolling them in a towel and gently squeezing. With a little care, most fresh herbs can be

refrigerated in the crisper drawer for a week or more. Wrap loosely in paper towels, then place in a plastic bag. Some fresh herbs, such as cilantro, mint and parsley have edible stems. We like to use them to flavor stocks, soups and stews. As for dried herbs, we rarely use them. They lack much of the nuance of fresh and generally require long, steady cooking to coax out their flavors. Exceptions to that rule include oregano (both Mexican and Turkish varieties, which offer different flavors) and mint, which packs a deeper, earthier flavor than fresh.

SPICES

Despite their seeming durability, spices contain volatile oils and are perishable. For best flavor, we recommend buying whole spices in small quantities. It's easy to grind them as needed in a spice mill (a cheap blade-style coffee grinder works well) or a mortar and pestle. If purchasing ground spices, choose amounts you can consume within six months. Older, flat-tasting spices can be perked up with a quick toast in a hot skillet.

Aleppo Pepper

Fruity and only moderately spicy, coarsely ground Aleppo pepper is used throughout Middle Eastern cooking. We use it frequently and consider it a valuable flavoring for dishes that benefit from a little spark of heat. For a quick substitute mix 2 teaspoons sweet paprika with 1 teaspoon red pepper flakes, rubbing with your fingers to crush the pepper flakes. Aleppo pepper can be found at most Middle Eastern shops and spice dealers. It's typically processed with a little salt and safflower oil.

Allspice

With a flavor tasting subtly of cinnamon, clove, nutmeg and black pepper, allspice works in both sweet and savory dishes. We typically buy whole allspice berries and grind them fresh for the best flavor. We also use whole allspice berries when pickling, though the berries should be removed before serving.

Bay Leaves

We think of bay leaves as we do of vanilla—it's a flavor noticed mostly by omission. Bay leaves lend a certain aroma and savory note to soups, stews and pickles. They're also great tossed with roasted vegetables (just be sure to remove them before serving). We even use them in syrups and sweets. Turkish bay leaves, which come from laurel trees, contribute the best flavor; California bay leaves are from a different tree and have a harsher flavor. Buy in bulk for economy's sake and store in the freezer to maintain flavor and aroma.

Black Pepper

Black pepper adds depth and nominal heat to dishes. We use it to give a mild kick—and not always hand-in-hand with salt. For best flavor, buy whole peppercorns and grind as needed (find a good-quality adjustable pepper mill). Pre-ground pepper lacks the aroma and much of the flavor of freshly ground. Consider tasting different varieties of black pepper to see which you prefer, as some are more aggressive than others.

Cardamom

Cardamom might be Milk Street's favorite spice. We use it widely in both sweet and savory recipes. It is sold whole in pods (white, black and green—each with a slightly different flavor), corticated (removed from the papery husk) and ground. More often than not, we use ground, as it can be difficult to grind finely. We also like to make Arabic coffee by grinding the whole pods into our coffee beans, then brewing as normal. Use 1 tablespoon of cardamom pods per 1 cup of whole coffee beans.

Coriander

Coriander is the seed of the cilantro plant. It has a bright, citrusy flavor with a hint of mint. The seeds are tender enough to use whole, though it is typically used ground. We prefer to buy it whole and grind as needed.

Cumin

One of our more liberally used spices, cumin packs an earthy flavor and pungency that lends backbone to all manner of Latin, Middle Eastern and even Indian dishes. Buy whole and grind fresh, if possible.

Dried Chilies

Dried chilies are used in many cuisines to add complexity and heat. Latin varieties tend to be the easiest to find. New Mexico chilies are perhaps the most common and most adaptable in flavor. Look for glossy, pliant-looking chilies in the Latin section of your grocer. We recommend pulling the stems off and shaking them out before using; the seeds can be bitter and overly spicy. Depending on the recipe, the chilies should be toasted or fried to deepen the flavor. Ancho chilies—which have a deep, almost prune-like flavor and mild spiciness—are interchangeable with pasilla chilies. Tangy, very fruity guajillo chilies taste hot and bright; they pair well with tomatoes and can be substituted for New Mexico chilies. Chipotle chilies are smoked red jalapeños; chipotle chilies en adobo, sold in cans, are the chilies packed in a tomato-vinegar sauce. The latter are often used in our recipes to add both smoke and spice. Pointy little árbol chilies can be quite hot; simmer them whole in a dish and pull them out before serving.

Fennel Seeds

We use both whole and ground fennel seeds to add a licorice-like flavor to meats, vegetables and sauces. Fennel pairs well with coriander and chili flakes.

Mustard Seeds

We pickle them or stir them into curries and the occasional bean dish for a pop of flavor. We prefer brown, though yellow mustard seeds are fine, too. Mustard seeds can be found in the spice section of most markets, either packaged or in bulk bins.

Nutmeg

The warm, sharp flavor of ground nutmeg works in sweet and savory dishes, both on its own and blended with other warm spices. It's especially important in cream sauces and often paired with lemon. The flavor is particularly volatile, so it is best to buy whole nutmeg and grate fresh as needed. A wand-style grater works well for this.

Paprika

Paprika adds deep, sweet and earthy flavor to countless dishes. It also has a bit of a thickening property when used in soups, stews and sauces. All paprika is made from dried red peppers. Whether it's hot or sweet depends on the variety of pepper used and if the seeds were removed. Though paprika originated in Latin America, it is often associated with Hungary or Spain. Hungarian paprika tends to be the most flavorful; it's usually identified as sweet or hot on the package. Smoked paprika is made from peppers that are slow-dried over a fire; we prefer pimentón de La Vera, which is produced only in the La Vera region of Spain. We use all types of paprika, depending on the flavor profile that we are aiming for in the recipe.

Red Pepper Flakes

The sharp bite of red pepper flakes serves to punctuate many dishes. We don't aim for spicy food per se, just balanced dishes with a compelling range of flavors to keep things interesting start to finish. Red pepper flakes are produced from various dried peppers, and intensity can vary from brand to brand. Age affects heat level as well; the older the flakes, the less intense they will be.

Salt

We use kosher salt in our cooking and baking because the larger granules are easier to measure and sprinkle with your fingers. The two most common brands are Diamond Crystal Kosher Salt and Morton Coarse Kosher Salt; we use the former. Grains of Diamond Crystal are slightly larger and fluffier than those of Morton, which are dense and compact, so the same volume of Diamond is less salty than Morton. If you use Morton in our recipes, reduce the amount called for to just over half. Flaky finishing salts, such as Maldon Sea Salt Flakes, add a delicious crunch and salty pop but should be used only at the table, not during cooking.

Shichimi Togarashi

One of our favorite seasoning blends is shichimi togarashi, a seven-ingredient mix that includes chili peppers, sesame seeds, citrus peel, seaweed and sometimes black peppercorns, poppy seeds and hemp seeds. We use the mix to enliven Japanese noodle dishes. It's also great as a seasoning for scrambled or fried eggs, broiled fish or chicken, or even roasted vegetables. Look for shichimi togarashi, sold in small glass bottles, in the international foods section of your grocer or an Asian specialty market.

Sichuan Peppercorns

Not technically pepper, Sichuan peppercorns have a sharp flavor and unique ability to "numb" the mouth. They are used broadly in Sichuan cooking in tandem with whole chilies in a combination known as "ma la." Make sure to sort well and remove the black seeds, which can contribute a gritty texture.

Sumac

Deep red and bursting with zesty flavor, sumac has been an essential flavoring of Middle Eastern cooking—and, closer to home, Native American cooking—for centuries. It's made from the berries of the sumac bush and is usually sold ground. You can find it online, at Middle Eastern markets and at some larger grocers. (Though they're related, this is not the poison sumac you've been warned to stay away from in the wild.) Sumac has a sour, lemony flavor and is a good way to add a bright pop of color and a tart note of citrus without the liquid of lemon juice. It works well as a condiment and can be dusted over just about anything—hummus and baba ghanoush are traditional, but it also makes a good popcorn topper. And it's good in dry rubs for chicken and fish.

White Pepper

While we use white pepper less than black, its unique flavor and pungent aroma make it an important pantry staple for some Scandinavian and Asian dishes. It comes from the same berry (pepper nigrum) as black, but is processed differently. Like black pepper, white is best when freshly ground. For a complex flavor, use a blend of black and white peppercorns in your pepper mill.

SEASONINGS

Anchovies

Few ingredients are as polarizing as anchovies. We love them and use them often. The best come jarred, though canned will suffice. Skip those rolled around a caper. And forget about anchovy paste—it may be convenient, but the poor-quality, salty flavor isn't worth it. Buy a jar of anchovies and keep it in the back of the refrigerator to add to sauces, soups and vegetables. Once they're heated and dissolved into a dish, they add tremendous savory flavor, but you'll never detect anything "fishy."

Chili Sauces

We use a variety of hot sauces in our cooking; you should taste different varieties to figure out which suits your heat threshold. We like Dynasty Thai Chili Garlic Paste. For a general Southeast Asian-style sauce, there are many Sriracha sauces ranging in potency; Shark brand Thai Sriracha Chili Sauce is milder, sweeter and tangier than most.

Dried Mushrooms

Umami-rich dried mushrooms pack a flavor punch well above their weight. For the most part, we use dried shiitake mushrooms, which add deep, savory flavor. To use them, dust them off, then soak them in hot water to soften before slicing and adding to dishes. Sometimes we add them whole to stocks and soups. They can also be ground to a powder and used in stews and sautés to add umami flavor without mushroom texture.

Fish Sauce

Fish sauce is just that: the fermented broth of salted, aged fish. The heady, amber-colored liquid is used throughout Southeast Asia as a seasoning, as well as for the base of countless sauces. We use it beyond Asian cuisines to add deep flavor to sauces. Brands vary widely in flavor. After tasting our way through a host of options, we found Red Boat Fish Sauce to be the best. It costs more than other brands, but the clean, rich flavor makes it well worth it. And a little goes a long way.

Kimchi

Kimchi—a spicy, pungent mix of fermented cabbage and other vegetables—has been an essential part of Korean cooking for more than 2,000 years. It began as a way to preserve food without refrigeration. The red and relatively fiery version has become more common in the U.S. as interest in Korean food has risen. You'll often find jars of it in the grocer's refrigerated section. But kimchi can also be quite mild and even white; there are more than 100 varieties. It usually contains a seafood element, such as fish sauce for flavoring. Served as a small plate at just about every Korean meal, kimchi can be offered as a vegetable side dish or pickle-like accompaniment to a main dish, or it can be used as a cooking ingredient. It stores well in the refrigerator, but its flavor becomes sharper and tangier over time.

Miso

Miso is fermented soybean paste, and there are many varieties, from white and smooth to dark and chunky. Two versions commonly found in the U.S. are shiro (white), which has a mild, sweet-and-salty flavor, and shinshu (yellow), which is fermented a little longer than shiro but still has a delicate flavor and light golden color. Red miso, fermented longer than shiro or shinshu, is saltier and works best where a heartier flavor is desired. The classic use of miso is in soup, though it can add a shot of umami to many dishes. Try white or yellow miso in sauces and dressings. One of our favorite ways to use miso is blended with an equal amount of softened butter and, if you like, grated fresh ginger. This mixture is terrific tossed with pasta for a carbonara-like dish or used to dress roasted or grilled vegetables.

Peppadew Peppers

A little sweet, a little tart, a little spicy, Peppadews are bright red, pleasantly spicy peppers that are about the size of a cherry tomato. They are a trademarked brand that originated in South Africa. The peppers are now widely available at grocers, usually jarred, but sometimes sold loose at the olive bar. Use the peppers to add mild piquancy to a salad, as part of an antipasto spread, as a pizza topping or as a companion to cheese. Peppadews are sold in mild, hot and golden varieties; we most often use mild.

Soy Sauce

Called soy sauce in China and shoyu in Japan, the inky-dark sauce is made from fermented, salted soybeans and typically a bit of wheat. It has a deep, umami-rich flavor; we use it frequently in both Asian and Western cooking. Soy sauce comes in a variety of styles. For the most part, we use regular soy sauce. "Light" soy sauce is a lighter color from the first pressing. It's light only in color; the flavor is salty and strong. Tamari is a Japanese variety that is often wheat-free (check the label). If sodium is an issue, choose a reduced-sodium version. "White" soy sauce is a high-end variety that should be used only as a dipping sauce. Sweet soy sauce, sometimes known as kecap manis, is soy sauce sweetened with molasses or palm sugar. It's not an appropriate substitute.

Tamarind

Tamarind is an intensely tart fruit used to add sour flavors in the cooking of Latin America, the Indian subcontinent and Southeast Asia. While some supermarkets sell whole tamarind pods—which look like long brown, leathery seed-pods—it's most often found as a jarred concentrate or a semi-dried block of pulp. We prefer the latter for its clearer, stronger flavor. To use, cut off a chunk of the sticky, dark pulp and soak in hot water to soften, about 10 minutes. Stir to loosen and discard the large seeds, then force the pulp through a fine-mesh strainer. We use the tangy, slightly molasses-y juice in dipping sauces, but it also adds a pleasant tartness to a variety of sauces, dressings and even cocktails. Try adding a splash to a gin and tonic, or do as Portland, Oregon's Pok Pok restaurant does and use it in a whiskey sour.

Za'atar

Za'atar can refer to two things—a dried herb and an herb blend that contains it. Both are used widely in Middle Eastern cooking. The plant is reminiscent of wild thyme and oregano. The herb blend comes in many varieties, differing by region and cook. Most contain the za'atar herb, as well as sesame seeds and other spices, such as sumac. The blend is often used as a substitute for lemon or vinegar where a liquid won't work. Za'atar can be found in Middle Eastern markets, better-stocked grocers or online. It can be mixed into olive oil and spread onto flatbread as one would butter, or swirled into labneh (yogurt cheese) with vinegar and oil. It can also be baked into bread, sprinkled on salads, pizza or hummus, or rubbed into meat and vegetables.

SWEETENERS

Whenever possible, we try to use sweeteners that contribute depth and flavor beyond sweetness.

Agave

A honey-like syrup made from the agave plant, agave has a clean, simple flavor and blends easily into other liquids, making it ideal for vinaigrettes and sauces. It can be purchased in a variety of shades, from light to dark. The lighter varieties are a good substitute for simple syrup in cocktails.

Brown Sugar

We like brown sugar because it adds earthy, caramel flavors that contribute so much more than basic sweetness. It may look like "raw" sugar, but it is really just white sugar blended with molasses. Light brown sugar has less molasses; dark brown has more (and consequently is more acidic).

Honey

We use honey in both sweet and savory dishes. In addition to its flavor, we like to take advantage of its hygroscopic (moisture-retaining) properties. This helps keep baked goods tender, but it also can prevent vegetables and other foods from drying out. As a general rule, we favor mild-flavored honeys, such as clover, which combine well with other flavors. Honey with assertive flavors, such as buckwheat and orange blossom, can compete with the other ingredients.

Palm Sugar

Produced from the sap of coconut palm trees, palm sugar has a creamy mouthfeel and earthy taste slightly reminiscent of maple sugar. It's used as a sweetener throughout Asia and is easily found at Asian markets. Light brown sugar is a good substitute.

STARCHES

All-Purpose Flour

For cooking and general baking, we prefer all-purpose flour with a lower protein level to ensure tender cookies and crisp pie dough. Brands we like include Gold Medal and Bob's Red Mill.

Bread Flour

High-protein bread flour is the best choice for chewy flatbreads and hearty loaves and boules. Don't substitute it for all-purpose, as it will make your pancakes and muffins dense and tough.

Graham Flour

Graham flour is coarse-ground whole-wheat flour. We like using it in cookies and breads because it can contribute a strong, wheaty flavor without the gumminess of finer whole-wheat flour. Look for it in natural foods stores or in bulk bins at a co-op. It is perishable and should be stored in the refrigerator or freezer. To intensify the flavor of graham flour, toast it in a dry skillet until it darkens.

Potato Starch

Potato starch is essential for the crisp texture of Korean pancakes and worth keeping around to use as a dusting for a variety of fried foods, such as chicken and fish. Look for potato starch in the baking aisle or Jewish foods section of the grocery store or at Asian markets. Note: Potato flour is different and should not be substituted.

Rye Flour

Rye flour has a slightly spicy, earthy flavor that we use to add complexity and a pleasant bitterness to baked goods. Try substituting it for a small amount of the all-purpose flour in pizza dough and pancakes for more complex flavor (no more than a 20 percent swap; otherwise the texture will be affected). Rye flour is more perishable than wheat flour and should be stored in the refrigerator or freezer.

Semolina Flour

Semolina is a coarse protein-rich flour produced from hard durum wheat. It's most commonly used to make dried pasta, and we also use it for dusting a peel for transferring pizza dough. In Italy and the Middle East, it turns up in recipes for cookies and sweets that benefit from a bit of added texture.

GRAINS & PASTA

Asian Noodles

There are dozens of varieties of Asian noodles made from an array of starches. Most Asian wheat noodles are made from a lower-protein wheat than is used for Italian pasta, so they tend to be softer and chewier. In our experience, udon noodles are the most widely available of this style. Japanese soba noodles are made with buckwheat and are brownish-gray in color, with nutty, mineral notes. If you can't find any Asian wheat noodles, substitute dried Italian linguine or fettuccine.

Bulgur

Chewy and firm with a nutty flavor, bulgur is an ancient ingredient. Though often confused with plain cracked wheat, which is uncooked, bulgur is a cooked and dried cracked wheat. It is made by boiling wheat berries, usually durum (a hard protein-rich wheat), until they are about to crack open, then allowing them to dry. The outer bran layers are rubbed off, and the grains are ground in grades ranging from fine to coarse. Preparation can be as simple as a cold soak (for fine) to a gentle simmer (for coarse). As with many grains, bulgur can be toasted to intensify its flavor. If you can't find fine-grain bulgur, process coarse bulgur in a spice grinder in short pulses until fine, light and fluffy, six to 10 pulses.

Italian Pasta

We always keep on hand a package of long, thin noodles—such as spaghetti or linguine—to use with creamy or thin sauces, as well as a pack of short or round stocky noodles—such as penne, gemelli or orecchiette—for chunkier sauces. Most of our pasta recipes are designed to use 12 ounces (3 ounces per serving—Italian-style), 4 ounces less than the average box of pasta. Either cook the extra pasta and save for the next day (terrific fried crisp in olive oil and topped with grated Parmesan and a fried egg), or save the surplus for a future batch. We like using tongs for stirring pasta; it makes it easy to separate any stuck pieces.

Rice

For pilafs and day-to-day eating, we like long-grain white rice. For Southeast Asian dishes, long-grain jasmine rice is ideal (note that U.S.-grown jasmine lacks the aroma and flavor of Asian-grown rice). For Indian dishes, long, thin grains of basmati are best. Rice is easy to make, though it does take a bit of time. For convenience, we often make a batch or two ahead and freeze it in zip-close bags. It thaws in just minutes in the microwave.

WINE & SPIRITS

Dry Sherry

Dry sherry is frequently used in Chinese cooking as a good substitute for hard-to-find Shaoxing cooking wine. It adds a sweet-sharp flavor that rounds out the herbs and ginger in the broth and works wonders on the flavor of the chicken. It's not necessary to spend much on a bottle. Palo cortado is a good varietal (a good bit cheaper than manzanilla or fino), and the Lustau brand is a reliable choice.

Mirin

Mirin is Japanese sweet rice wine. Aji-mirin varieties are sweetened with added sugar and sometimes seasoned with salt; hon-mirin varieties have no added sugar (and are more expensive). As with many things, the more you spend, the better the quality. Lower-quality varieties are made largely from corn syrup and flavorings. We prefer hon-mirin when available.

Rye Whiskey

The spicy flavors of rye are particularly well suited to flavoring spiced baked goods. Among good brands for cooking, Rittenhouse Rye packs a lot of spice and doesn't cost a fortune (and it makes a great Manhattan).

Rum

We use the spicy, earthy flavor of dark rum in some baking because it does a terrific job of accenting spices, vanilla and brown sugar. Myers's Rum Original Dark and Gosling's Black Seal Bermuda Black Rum are excellent choices for cooking.

Vermouth

Vermouth is wine fortified with additional alcohol and flavored with a variety of botanicals. The herbal notes of vermouth make it particularly well suited for pairing with vegetables, poultry and seafood. An opened bottle of vermouth stores well for up to a month in the refrigerator. For cooking, be sure to use dry vermouth; sweet vermouth is best in a Manhattan or negroni.

Wine

The basic rule for selecting a cooking wine: Don't spend a fortune, but do make sure it's drinkable. When choosing wines to cook with, look for neutral, dry varietals and blends. For whites, we stick with sauvignon blanc, pinot gris, Côtes du Rhône and Spanish Rueda wines. Avoid anything oaky, such as chardonnay, or overly aromatic, like riesling and gewürztraminer. For reds, we like Côtes du Rhône again, as well as grenache and syrah. If you have leftover drinking wine that won't be consumed within a few days, consider simmering it down until it reduces by half, then freeze it in an ice cube tray. It's a quick way to add big flavor to soups, stews, stocks and sauces.

Eggs

2

A SLICKER SCRAMBLE

We were won over the first time we tried cooking scrambled eggs in oil. They were almost instantly cooked in rolling, variegated waves and came out fresh and light, not greasy or heavy.

Why? Oil gets hotter faster than butter. That's because butter is 20 percent water and can exceed 212°F only once the water has evaporated. Further, the proteins in eggs are folded. Heat unfolds (denatures) them, creating a network that traps the steam given off as the eggs cook. Extra-virgin olive oil is unique among vegetable oils since it contains surfactants (surface-area agents) that make it easier for that network to form. All of that means you have oil getting hotter more quickly and making more steam faster along with a protein network that traps that steam better. Result: Quicker, bigger puffs and more impressive scrambled eggs.

Fluffy Olive Oil **Scrambled Eggs**

Start to finish: **10 minutes** / Servings: 4

We'd never questioned the French rule that butter is best for cooking eggs. But then we noticed that chefs at hotel breakfast stations use oil to make omelets in carbon-steel pans. Likewise, the Chinese cook their well-seasoned, well-browned omelets in oil, as do the Japanese. But scrambled eggs? As a test, we heated olive oil until just smoking and poured in whisked eggs. Whoosh! In a quick puff of steam, we had light, fluffy eggs. The oil needed a full 3 minutes at medium heat to get hot enough. Higher temperatures cooked the eggs too fast, toughening them. Two tablespoons of oil was enough to coat the bottom of the skillet and flavor the eggs without making them greasy. We like our scrambled eggs particularly wet and not entirely cooked through, which takes just 30 seconds. Leave them a little longer for drier eggs. Either way, take them off the heat before they are fully cooked and let them rest on a warm plate for 30 seconds. They finish cooking off the heat. Mixing the salt into the eggs before cooking was the best way to season them.

Don't warm your plates too much. It sounds minor, but hot plates will continue to cook the eggs, making them tough and dry. Cold plates will cool the eggs too fast. The plates should be warm to the touch, but not so hot that you can't comfortably hold them.

FLUFFY OLIVE OIL SCRAMBLED EGGS

2 tablespoons extra-virgin olive oil

8 large eggs

Kosher salt and ground black pepper

1. In a 12-inch nonstick or seasoned carbon-steel skillet over medium, heat the oil until just starting to smoke, about 3 minutes. While the oil heats, in a bowl, use a fork to whisk the eggs and ¾ teaspoon salt until blended and foamy. Pour the eggs into the center of the pan.

2. Using a rubber spatula, continuously stir the eggs, pushing them toward the middle as they set at the edges and folding the cooked egg over on itself. Cook until just set, 60 to 90 seconds. The curds should be shiny, wet and soft, but not translucent or runny. Immediately transfer to warmed plates. Season with salt and pepper.

SUNNY-SIDE UP FRIED EGGS

Start to finish: **8 minutes**
Makes 4 eggs

Hot oil gave us the best scrambled eggs, but fried eggs turned out to be a different game. Here, butter truly was better; oil produced tough, greasy fried eggs. Every stovetop has a different low setting, and skillets vary in thickness and heat conductivity. It may take a few attempts to determine the best timing for your equipment. For us, 3 minutes was perfect for completely set whites and thick but runny yolks. If you like very loose yolks, shave off a minute; for lightly browned whites and firm yolks, add a minute. To make 2 eggs, use an 8-inch skillet and 2 teaspoons of butter.

Don't break the yolks when cracking the eggs into the bowl. If you're not confident in your egg-cracking skills, break the eggs one at a time into a small bowl before combining them.

4 large eggs

1 tablespoon salted butter

Kosher salt and ground black pepper

1. Heat a 10-inch nonstick skillet over low for 3 minutes. Crack the eggs into a bowl. Add the butter to the hot pan and swirl until melted. When the butter stops foaming, slowly pour the eggs into the skillet. If necessary, gently nudge the yolks with a wooden spoon to space them evenly in the pan.

2. Working quickly, season the eggs with salt and pepper, then cover the skillet and cook until the whites are completely set and the yolks are bright yellow, about 3 minutes. Slide out of the pan and onto plates.

WELL-SEASONED STEEL

Chefs love carbon-steel pans, and for good reason. These pans are inexpensive, rugged, heat evenly and retain heat well. Best yet, they can develop a natural nonstick coating without the worrying chemicals of typical nonstick surfaces. Turns out, they're handy for home cooks, too.

First, you need to master the (simple) art of seasoning the pans, a process that coats them with oil and heats the oil to high temperatures. This causes the oil to polymerize, or form long chains of molecules that bond to the metal. That bonding means there are fewer iron molecules available to bond with the food. And no bonding means no sticking.

Most methods call for seasoning skillets just after buying them. We do this, but got even better results by adding a trick cooks at Chinese restaurants use to keep woks (often made of carbon steel) slick. Every time they cook, they ladle oil into the hot pan to coat it, then dump it out before adding fresh oil for cooking. This fills any divots in the coating caused by daily wear.

We didn't find huge differences in brands of carbon-steel pans. It was the seasoning that made the difference. Most 10-inch pans—a practical size for home cooking—can be purchased for less than $25.

INITIAL SEASONING: Scrub the pan with hot soapy water, then dry and set over medium heat. Use a paper towel held with tongs to spread 1 tablespoon vegetable oil evenly over the pan. Leave on the heat until it smokes, then hold it at that stage for 1 minute. Use a paper towel held with tongs to wipe the pan clean. Repeat the process until the pan develops a golden-brown patina, three to five repetitions. The pan may look blotchy, but will even out with use.

DAILY USE: Set the pan over medium heat and add 1 teaspoon of vegetable oil. Use a paper towel held with tongs to wipe the oil evenly over the pan. When the oil smokes, hold it at that stage for 1 minute, then wipe clean with another paper towel held with tongs. Allow the pan to cool for 3 to 5 minutes, then add the oil or butter for cooking. Don't skip the cooling step or the pan will be too hot and burn the cooking fat.

DAILY CARE: Treat your seasoned pan well. Never plunge a hot carbon-steel pan into cold water; the thermal shock can crack the pan. And avoid soap; it will dissolve the seasoning. After cooking, clean the pan with a wet sponge (and a little coarse salt mixed with oil if needed to scrub away stubborn bits), dry it well and wipe lightly with oil before storing.

Baked Persian Herb Omelet
(*Kuku Sabzi*)

Start to finish: **1 hour** (20 minutes active) / Servings: 6

5 tablespoons extra-virgin olive oil, divided

2 cups lightly packed fresh flat-leaf parsley leaves

2 cups lightly packed fresh cilantro leaves and tender stems

1 cup coarsely chopped fresh dill

6 scallions, trimmed and coarsely chopped

1½ teaspoons baking powder

1 teaspoon kosher salt

¾ teaspoon ground cardamom

¾ teaspoon ground cinnamon

½ teaspoon ground cumin

¼ teaspoon ground black pepper

6 large eggs

½ cup walnuts, toasted and chopped (optional)

⅓ cup dried cranberries, coarsely chopped (optional)

Whole-milk Greek-style yogurt, to serve (optional)

As France claims the omelet, Italy the frittata and Spain the tortilla, Iran has kuku, a baked egg dish. The kuku sabzi variation gets its flavor—and a deep green color—from tons of fresh herbs. We love this approach to fresh herbs. Using heaps of them delivers big flavor effortlessly, and keeps heavy dishes feeling light and fresh. Kuku sabzi—which is served at Persian New Year's feasts—remains light despite six eggs and a handful of walnuts (for texture and richness) thanks to five cups of parsley, cilantro and dill. Also helping is baking powder, which forms tiny air bubbles that catch the steam released as the eggs cook, causing the dish to rise. While some recipes for kuku sabzi opt for stovetop cooking (with copious oil), we preferred the ease of baking. Pulsing the herbs and scallions in the food processor was easier and faster than hand chopping, and the texture was better. Dried cranberries were a good stand-in for traditional Persian barberries—lending a sweet-and-savory balance—but the recipe works without them.

Don't use less than 2 tablespoons of oil to grease the pan; the oil should pool at the bottom and generously coat the sides. This crisps the edges and boosts the omelet's flavor.

1. Heat the oven to 375°F with a rack in the upper-middle position. Coat the bottom and sides of an 8-inch square or 9-inch round cake pan with 2 tablespoons of the oil. Line the bottom of the pan with a square of kitchen parchment, then turn the parchment to coat both sides with oil.

2. In a food processor, combine the parsley, cilantro, dill, scallions and the remaining 3 tablespoons oil. Process until finely ground. In a large bowl, whisk together the baking powder, salt, cardamom, cinnamon, cumin and pepper. Add 2 of the eggs and whisk until blended. Add the remaining 4 eggs and whisk until just combined. Fold in the herb-scallion mixture and the walnuts and cranberries, if using. Pour into the prepared pan and smooth the top. Bake until the center is firm, 20 to 25 minutes.

3. Let the kuku cool in the pan on a rack for 10 minutes. Run a knife around the edges, then invert onto a plate and remove the parchment. Reinvert onto a cutting board or serving platter. Cut into wedges and serve warm, cold or room temperature with a dollop of yogurt, if desired. The kuku can be refrigerated for up to 3 days, tightly wrapped.

Curry Braised Eggs

Start to finish: 1 hour 15 minutes (50 minutes active) / Servings: 4

3 tablespoons grapeseed or other neutral oil

1 large yellow onion, halved and thinly sliced lengthwise

Kosher salt

2 tablespoons finely grated fresh ginger

4 teaspoons garam masala

1 teaspoon ground turmeric

¼ teaspoon cayenne pepper

Three 14½-ounce cans diced tomatoes, drained

14-ounce can coconut milk

1 tablespoon packed brown sugar

Ground black pepper

1 tablespoon lime juice, plus lime wedges to serve

8 large eggs

⅓ cup chopped fresh cilantro

Steamed basmati rice, naan or boiled potatoes, to serve (optional)

Eggs are bit players in Western dinners. We eat them for breakfast and brunch, but come evening they rarely appear except as accessories for the put-an-egg-on-it crowd. The rest of the world knows better. Portugal, for example, has ervilhas com ovos, braised eggs with spicy or sweet Portuguese chourico sausage and/or bacon and peas. In India, there is muttai kuzhambu, a type of egg curry. Both dishes are built on layers of seasoning that balance the richness of the eggs. We liked the way garam masala—a warmly flavored Indian seasoning blend—added complex flavor. For our vegetables, we started with onions and found that sliced worked better than diced, adding texture and helping the sauce hold its shape. We let the sauce cool a bit in the dish before adding the eggs to ensure even cooking. While we like runny yolks, feel free to leave the dish in the oven a bit longer for firm yolks.

Don't forget that every oven is different, not to mention every egg. Cooking times will depend on oven temperature, as well as the size and temperature of the eggs.

1. Heat the oven to 375°F with a rack in the lower-middle position. In a 6- to 8-quart Dutch oven over medium, heat the oil. Add the onion and ½ teaspoon salt. Cook, stirring, until browned, 7 to 9 minutes. Add the ginger, garam masala, turmeric and cayenne. Cook for 30 seconds, stirring constantly. Add the tomatoes, coconut milk, sugar, ¾ teaspoon salt and ½ teaspoon pepper. Bring to a boil, scraping up any browned bits. Reduce heat to medium and simmer, stirring and scraping the pan, until thickened, 20 to 25 minutes.

2. Remove the pan from the heat and let sit for 10 minutes, stirring occasionally. Stir in the lime juice, then taste and season with salt and pepper. Use the back of a spoon to make 8 evenly spaced wells in the sauce. Crack 1 egg into each well, then season the eggs with salt and pepper.

3. Bake until the sauce is bubbling and the egg whites are opaque but still jiggle slightly, 13 to 18 minutes, rotating the pot halfway through. Remove from the oven and let sit for 5 minutes. Sprinkle with cilantro and serve with lime wedges and rice, naan or potatoes, if desired.

Spanish-Style Eggs with Garlicky Crumbs and Chorizo (*Migas*)

Start to finish: **30 minutes** / Servings: 4

8 large eggs

Kosher salt

3 ounces Spanish chorizo, halved lengthwise and thinly sliced crosswise

3 tablespoons extra-virgin olive oil, divided

2½ cups ½-inch chewy bread cubes

1 medium red onion, diced (about 1 cup)

2 garlic cloves, thinly sliced

¼ teaspoon sweet paprika

¼ teaspoon cayenne pepper (optional)

4 cups lightly packed coarsely chopped lacinato kale (about 3 ounces)

Ground black pepper

Migas evolved as a Spanish-Portuguese dish intended to use up stale bread. In fact, the word is Spanish for crumbs. Traditionally, the bread is torn into cubes, sprinkled with water and left overnight. Since most Americans don't have stale bread sitting around, we used ½-inch cubes of rustic bread. The best way to flavor them was to toss them in garlicky oil before toasting them in a skillet. We used Spanish-style chorizo, which is cured, and added a diced red onion along with chopped fresh kale. Lacinato (dinosaur) kale gave the dish heft, color and flavor. Be sure to stem the kale before measuring or weighing it, or substitute baby kale, which requires no stemming. For a variation, reduce or omit the kale and add 1 cup of chopped roasted red peppers or frozen peas (thawed). We found the bread cubes worked best when stirred in at the end of cooking, which gave them a chance to reheat and just begin to soften at the edges without losing their crunch. Their salty, garlicky flavor came through beautifully.

Don't walk away while browning the chorizo. Chorizo brands vary widely in fat content—not to mention flavor—and can go from golden brown to burnt in seconds.

1. In a medium bowl, whisk the eggs and ½ teaspoon salt. In a 12-inch non-stick skillet over medium, cook the chorizo, stirring frequently, until browned and crisp, 2 to 5 minutes. Use a slotted spoon to transfer the chorizo to a medium bowl, leaving any fat in the pan.

2. Add 2 tablespoons of the olive oil to the skillet and return to medium-high. Add the bread and a pinch of salt, then cook, stirring and tossing frequently, until browned and crisp, 3 to 5 minutes. Transfer to the bowl with the chorizo.

3. Return the skillet to medium heat and add the remaining 1 tablespoon oil, the onion, garlic, paprika, cayenne, if using, and ¼ teaspoon salt. Cook,

stirring frequently, until the onion and garlic are softened and lightly browned, 3 to 5 minutes. If the garlic darkens too fast, reduce the heat. Add the kale and cook until wilted but still bright green, 1 to 2 minutes.

4. Whisk the eggs to recombine, then pour into the skillet and immediately reduce the heat to low. Cook, stirring and scraping the edges of the pan constantly, until barely set, about 1 minute. Stir in the bread and chorizo. Cook to desired consistency, 30 to 90 seconds. Transfer to a platter and season with salt and pepper.

Korean Scallion Pancakes (*Pajeon*)

Start to finish: 30 minutes / Servings: 4

65 grams (½ cup) all-purpose flour

½ cup potato starch

1 teaspoon red pepper flakes

1 teaspoon kosher salt

1 cup ice water

1 large egg, beaten

6 scallions, trimmed and
cut into 1-inch pieces

¼ cup shredded carrot
(about ½ medium carrot)

¼ cup soy sauce

3 tablespoons unseasoned
rice vinegar

½ teaspoon toasted sesame oil

¼ teaspoon ground black pepper

2 tablespoons grapeseed or
other neutral oil, divided

Quick to make and with a crisp exterior but chewy center, pajeon take pancakes from breakfast to dinner. We tried several flour combinations in our search for just the right texture. We found that a combination of all-purpose flour and potato starch gave these pancakes their signature crisp-chewy texture. Using ice water in our batter encouraged the pancakes to puff while cooking, producing slightly crisped edges. Some recipes use as few as two scallions but we preferred more, settling on six. We started our pancake at a medium-high heat, but needed to reduce it after flipping to prevent the scallions from burning. If you can find gochugaru, or Korean chili powder, use it in place of the red pepper flakes for a sweeter, smokier flavor. Looking to switch up the flavors? We've included kimchi and seafood variations.

Don't use potato flour, which has a strong potato flavor and reacts differently with water. Bob's Red Mill makes potato starch, which is usually available in the baking aisle or natural foods section of your grocer.

1. In a medium bowl, whisk together the flour, potato starch, pepper flakes and salt. Add the water and egg and whisk until smooth. Fold in the scallions and carrots. Set aside. In a small bowl, combine the soy sauce, vinegar, sesame oil and pepper; set aside.

2. In a 12-inch nonstick skillet, heat 1 tablespoon of the grapeseed oil over medium-high until barely smoking. Stir the batter to recombine, then add half (1 scant cup) to the skillet, spreading it and the vegetables evenly to the edges of the pan. Cook until the top is set and the pancakes get lightly brown around the edges, 3 to 4 minutes.

3. Reduce heat to medium-low, then use a spatula to flip the pancake. Cook until golden brown on the second side, being careful not to burn the scallions, 1 to 2 minutes. Flip again and cook until

the pancake is charred in spots and crisp around the edges, 2 to 4 minutes. Transfer to a plate. Increase the heat to medium-high and repeat with the remaining 1 tablespoon grapeseed oil and the remaining batter. Cut the pancakes into wedges and serve with the sauce.

VARIATIONS:

For kimchi pancakes: Substitute ⅔ cup sliced napa cabbage kimchi for the scallions and carrots. Squeeze the kimchi gently before adding to remove excess liquid.

For seafood pancakes: Eliminate the carrot and add ½ cup chopped raw shrimp (peeled and deveined) to the batter with the scallions.

Turkish Scrambled Eggs with Spicy Tomato and Capers (*Menemen*)

Start to finish: **20 minutes** / Servings: 4

4 tablespoons extra-virgin olive oil, divided, plus more to serve

2 poblano chilies, stemmed, seeded and finely chopped

1 bunch scallions, thinly sliced

3 medium garlic cloves, minced

1 tablespoon Aleppo pepper or substitute, see p. 7

Kosher salt and ground white pepper

1 plum tomato, cored and finely chopped

2 tablespoons drained capers

8 large eggs

⅓ cup crumbled feta cheese

3 tablespoons chopped fresh dill

Poblano chilies are Mexican in heritage, but their earthy flavor and mild heat make them ideal for this version of Turkish-style scrambled eggs. Using Aleppo pepper nudges the dish closer to the traditional flavor profile, but if you don't have any, see p. 7 for a substitute. Serve on warmed plates to prevent the eggs from cooling too quickly. Round out the meal with crisp slices of toast.

Don't wait until the eggs are firm and fully set before removing the pan from the heat; the eggs continue to cook in the time it takes to portion and serve.

1. In a 12-inch nonstick skillet over medium, heat 2 tablespoons of oil until shimmering. Add the poblanos, scallions, garlic, Aleppo pepper and ½ teaspoon each salt and white pepper. Cover and cook, stirring, until the chilies are softened but not browned, 6 to 8 minutes. Transfer to a medium bowl and stir in the tomato and capers; set aside. Wipe out the skillet.

2. In a medium bowl, whisk the eggs and ¾ teaspoon salt. Return the skillet to medium and heat the remaining 2 tablespoons oil until shimmering. Pour the eggs into the center of the pan.

3. Using a silicone spatula, continuously stir the eggs, pushing them toward the middle as they set at the edges and folding the cooked egg over on itself. Cook until just set, about 1½ minutes. The curds should be shiny, wet and soft. Taste and season with salt and pepper, then divide among warmed serving plates.

4. Top each serving with a portion of the poblano mixture. Sprinkle with feta and dill, then drizzle with oil.

Soups

3

Miso-Shiitake Soup with Napa Cabbage

Start to finish: **30 minutes** / Servings: **6**

½ pound carrots (2 to 3 medium), peeled, halved lengthwise and cut crosswise into ½-inch pieces

2 tablespoons dried wakame seaweed

8 ounces soft tofu, drained and cut into ½-inch cubes

5 ounces fresh shiitake mushrooms, stems discarded, caps thinly sliced

4 cups chopped napa cabbage (½ small head)

6 tablespoons (3½ ounces) white miso paste

1-inch chunk fresh ginger, grated

1 tablespoon soy sauce, plus more to serve

2 teaspoons toasted sesame oil, plus more to serve

4 ounces (about 4 cups) baby spinach

6 scallions, trimmed and cut into 1-inch lengths

Hot chili oil, to serve (optional)

In Japan, where soup has evolved into high art, nabe (NAH-beh) is shorthand for nabemono, a broad category of soups that may be more recognizable by its Westernized name—hot pot. One such soup, yosenabe, loosely translates to "anything goes hot pot" and relies on layering flavors, adding them to the pot one at a time. Dense or long-cooking items go in first; more delicate ingredients follow. For our simplified yosenabe, we leaned heavily on vegetables. Most Japanese soups begin with dashi, a broth made from kombu seaweed and bonito, or shaved shreds of smoked tuna. We used more common but equally flavorful fresh shiitake mushrooms and dried wakame seaweed. (Wakame tastes slightly sweet and oceanic; look for it in the Asian foods aisle.) Timing was simple: Each ingredient cooked through in the time it took for the pot to return to a simmer. Yosenabe is typically flavored with a blend of soy sauce, sesame oil or scallions. We added all of them.

Don't use firm or extra-firm tofu in this recipe. Soft tofu had the best texture. Silken and medium tofu were decent substitutes.

1. In a medium Dutch oven over medium, combine 7 cups water, the carrots and wakame. Bring to a simmer and cook for 5 minutes. Add the tofu and mushrooms, then return to a simmer. Add the cabbage, then return to a simmer.

2. Place the miso in a 2-cup liquid measuring cup. Ladle out a bit of the cooking water and add to the miso, stirring until smooth. Pour the miso mixture back into the soup, then stir well.

3. As the soup returns to a simmer, stir in the ginger, soy sauce and sesame oil. Once the soup reaches a simmer, remove it from the heat and stir in the spinach and scallions. When the spinach is wilted, ladle the soup into serving bowls. Serve with soy sauce, sesame oil and chili oil, if using.

Turkish **Red Lentil Soup**

Start to finish: 45 minutes / Servings: 4

3 tablespoons salted butter

1 medium yellow onion, chopped

1 medium garlic clove, finely grated

1 tablespoon tomato paste

1 tablespoon sweet paprika

½ teaspoon ground cumin

1 cup red lentils

2 tablespoons long-grain white rice

Kosher salt

3 tablespoons extra-virgin olive oil

2 teaspoons Aleppo pepper (see note)

Chopped fresh mint, to serve (optional)

Lemon wedges, to serve

This simple yet substantial Turkish soup is made with red lentils, which soften and break down during cooking, adding texture. The Aleppo pepper brings gentle heat to the dish. If you can't find it locally, order online or see substitute, p. 7. The soup can be made vegan by substituting olive oil for the butter.

Don't omit the rice. The grains help thicken the soup.

1. In a large saucepan over medium, melt the butter. Add the onion and cook, stirring occasionally, until softened and translucent, about 5 minutes. Stir in the garlic and cook until fragrant, about 30 seconds. Stir in the tomato paste, paprika and cumin, then cook for about 1 minute.

2. Add the lentils, rice, 5 cups water and 2 teaspoons salt. Stir to combine and bring to a boil over medium-high. Reduce the heat to maintain a steady simmer, cover and cook, stirring occasionally, until the lentils and rice are tender and broken down, about 30 minutes. Season to taste.

3. Meanwhile, in a small skillet over medium, heat the olive oil, swirling to coat the pan. Add the Aleppo pepper and cook until a few bubbles appear and the oil is bright red, 1 to 2 minutes. Remove from the heat and set aside.

4. Serve the soup with Aleppo pepper oil drizzled over each serving and sprinkled with mint, if using, and lemon wedges on the side.

Chickpea and Harissa Soup (*Lablabi*)

Start to finish: 1 hour, plus soaking the chickpeas / Servings: 8

For the soup:

2 cups dried chickpeas

Kosher salt and ground black pepper

5 tablespoons extra-virgin olive oil, divided

1 large yellow onion, chopped

6 medium garlic cloves, minced

2 tablespoons tomato paste

2 tablespoons ground cumin, toasted

6 tablespoons harissa

3 quarts low-sodium chicken broth or water

8 ounces crusty white bread, sliced ½-inch-thick and torn into bite-size pieces

2 tablespoons lemon juice

For serving:

8 soft-cooked eggs, peeled and halved

½ cup drained capers

½ cup chopped pitted green olives

½ cup chopped fresh flat-leaf parsley

½ cup chopped fresh cilantro

Extra-virgin olive oil

Harissa

2 tablespoons ground cumin, toasted

Lemon wedges

This brothy-bready Tunisian chickpea soup gets punches of flavor from garlic, tomato paste and cumin. For the harissa, use our recipe (p. 362) or buy it ready-made; we like the DEA brand. And instead of using stale bread—as is common in Tunisia—we got better texture by toasting chunks of crusty bread in olive oil to make croutons. Toasted ground cumin is used in the soup as well as on it as a garnish; to be efficient, toast it all at once. In a small, dry skillet over medium, toast 5 tablespoons ground cumin, stirring constantly, until fragrant, about 1 minute, then transfer to a small bowl. To make soft-cooked eggs for serving, bring 2 cups water to a simmer in a large saucepan fitted with a steamer basket. Add the desired number of eggs, cover and steam over medium for 7 minutes. Immediately transfer to ice water to stop the cooking.

Don't forget to soak the dried chickpeas. They need to soak for at least 12 hours before cooking.

1. First, soak the chickpeas. In a large bowl, combine 2 quarts water, the chickpeas and 2 tablespoons salt. Let soak at room temperature for at least 12 hours or up to 24 hours. Drain the chickpeas and set aside.

2. To make the soup, in a large Dutch oven, heat 2 tablespoons of oil until shimmering. Add the onion and cook, stirring occasionally, until lightly golden, about 5 minutes. Stir in the garlic and cook until fragrant, about 30 seconds. Add the tomato paste and cook, stirring, until it browns, about 2 minutes. Stir in the cumin and harissa, then cook until fragrant, about 1 minute. Add the chickpeas and broth, then bring to a boil over high. Reduce to medium and simmer, uncovered, stirring occasionally, until the chickpeas are tender, about 1 hour.

3. Meanwhile, in a 12-inch nonstick skillet over medium, combine the bread, the remaining 3 tablespoons oil and 1 teaspoon salt. Cook, stirring occasionally, until crisp and light golden brown, 4 to 6 minutes. Remove from the heat and let the croutons cool in the pan. Transfer to a bowl.

4. When the chickpeas are tender, remove the pot from the heat and stir in the lemon juice. Taste and season with salt and pepper.

5. To serve, place 2 to 3 tablespoons of croutons in each serving bowl. Ladle chickpeas and broth around them, then top each portion with soft-cooked egg halves and 1 tablespoon each capers, olives, parsley and cilantro, or as desired. Drizzle with oil and garnish to taste with harissa and cumin. Serve with lemon wedges.

Korean Pork and Kimchi Stew (*Kimchi Jjigae*)

Start to finish: 1 hour 15 minutes (25 minutes active) / Servings: 6

1 cup boiling water,
plus 5 cups cold water

½ ounce dried shiitake mushrooms,
brushed clean

6 scallions, white parts finely
chopped, green parts thinly sliced
on diagonal, reserved separately

3 garlic cloves, smashed and peeled

1 tablespoon toasted sesame oil

1 tablespoon soy sauce

16-ounce container napa cabbage
kimchi, drained (¼ cup liquid
reserved) and coarsely chopped

4 teaspoons gochujang

1 pound baby back ribs, separated
into individual ribs

12 ounces medium-firm or firm tofu,
drained and cut into ¾-inch cubes

2 teaspoons white sugar

Looking for a stew with big flavor and easy prep, we were delighted to encounter Korean pork and kimchi stew. The assertively seasoned dish uses purchased kimchi—the pungent fermented cabbage that is a staple of Korean cooking—to easily add both vegetables and flavor. We built on our kimchi base with bone-in, baby back ribs for meaty flavor, cutting them into individual ribs so they tenderized quickly in the simmering broth. The bones and connective tissue of the ribs also add body to the broth. We layered the heat by combining another Korean favorite, gochujang chili paste, as well as the juice from the drained kimchi. For another time-saver, look for pre-sliced dried shiitake mushrooms. Serve with bowls of steamed white rice for a complete meal.

Don't use extra-firm or soft tofu. Soft or silken tofu was too fragile, and extra-firm added too much chew. Textures vary by brand, but we preferred medium-firm and firm.

1. In a small bowl, combine the boiling water and mushrooms. Let sit for 30 minutes.

2. Drain the mushrooms, reserving the soaking liquid. Discard the stems and thinly slice the caps. In a large Dutch oven over medium-high, combine the scallion whites, garlic, sesame oil and soy sauce. Cook, stirring occasionally, until the scallions have softened, 3 to 4 minutes. Stir in half of the kimchi, the sliced mushrooms and the gochujang. Add the cold water, the mushrooms' soaking liquid, the ribs and ¼ cup kimchi liquid and bring to a boil. Cover, leaving the lid slightly ajar, reduce the heat to medium-low and cook until rib meat is easily pierced with a knife, about 50 minutes, adjusting the heat to maintain a lively simmer.

3. Remove the pot from the heat. Using tongs, transfer the ribs to a plate and let rest until cool enough to handle, about 15 minutes.

4. Shred the meat into bite-size pieces, discarding the bones and cartilage. Add the meat to the stew along with the tofu, scallion greens, sugar and remaining kimchi. Bring to a simmer over medium and cook for 5 minutes.

Singapore Shrimp and Chicken Noodle Soup (*Laksa*)

Start to finish: **1 hour 20 minutes** / Servings: 6

6 medium shallots, peeled and halved

6 medium garlic cloves, peeled

3 tablespoons Thai red curry paste

2 lemon grass stalks, trimmed to the bottom 6 inches, dry outer layers discarded, chopped

2-inch piece fresh ginger, peeled and sliced into coins

2 teaspoons ground turmeric

1 bunch fresh cilantro, tender stems and leaves chopped, reserved separately, plus cilantro leaves, to serve

2 tablespoons grapeseed or other neutral oil

1 pound jumbo shrimp, peeled (shells reserved) and deveined

1 pound boneless, skinless chicken thighs, trimmed

14-ounce container firm tofu, drained, patted dry and cut into ½-inch cubes

6 tablespoons fish sauce, divided

3 tablespoons chili-garlic sauce, divided, plus more to serve

6 ounces wide (¼ inch) rice stick noodles

14-ounce can coconut milk

Kosher salt and ground white pepper

3 tablespoons lime juice, plus lime wedges, to serve

Laksa is a vibrant seafood and chicken noodle soup eaten from breakfast through dinner in Singapore. We use the shrimp shells to give maximum flavor to a broth that is seasoned with shallots, lemon grass and Thai red curry paste. You can boost the spiciness of the soup with extra chili-garlic sauce. If you like, garnish with chopped cucumber, halved hard-cooked eggs and chopped roasted peanuts.

Don't purchase shrimp that have been treated with sodium tripolyphosphate, an additive that improves the shrimps' appearance but also gives them an undesirable saltiness and unappealing texture. Check the label on the package or ask at the seafood counter. Don't discard the shrimp shells; you'll need them to make the broth. If you purchased already peeled shrimp, use just the tails for the broth.

1. In a food processor, combine the shallots, garlic, curry paste, lemon grass, ginger, turmeric and cilantro stems. Process until finely chopped, about 20 seconds.

2. In a large Dutch oven over medium-high, heat the oil until barely smoking. Add the shrimp shells and cook, stirring frequently, until they begin to char, 2 to 3 minutes. Stir in the shallot mixture and cook, stirring constantly, until fragrant and the paste begins to stick to the pot, about 2 minutes. Add 2 quarts water and bring to a boil over high, then reduce to medium-low, cover and simmer for 30 minutes.

3. Strain the broth through a fine mesh strainer set over a large heat-safe bowl, pressing on the solids to extract as much liquid as possible. Discard the solids. Return the broth to the pot and bring to a simmer over medium-high. Stir in the chicken, tofu, 1 tablespoon of fish sauce and 1 tablespoon of chili-garlic sauce. Return to a simmer, cover and reduce to low. Cook until a skewer inserted into the chicken meets no resistance, about 30 minutes.

4. Meanwhile, in a small bowl, toss the shrimp with 1 tablespoon of the remaining fish sauce and 1 tablespoon of the remaining chili-garlic sauce. Cover and refrigerate until needed.

5. Bring a large pot of water to a boil, then remove from the heat. Stir in the noodles and let soak until softened but still chewy, about 10 minutes. Drain in a colander, rinse under cold water and drain again. Divide the noodles evenly among 6 serving bowls.

6. When the chicken is cooked, transfer to a bowl, then use 2 forks to shred it into bite-size pieces. Return the chicken to the pot and stir in the coconut milk. Bring to a simmer over medium, then reduce to low. Add the shrimp and cook, stirring occasionally, until the shrimp are cooked through and opaque, 1 to 2 minutes.

7. Off heat, stir in the cilantro leaves, the remaining 4 tablespoons fish sauce, the remaining 1 tablespoon chili-garlic sauce and the lime juice. Taste and season with salt and white pepper. Ladle the soup over the noodles. Sprinkle with cilantro leaves and serve with lime wedges and chili-garlic sauce.

Pork and Vegetable Miso Soup (*Ton-Jiru*)

Start to finish: **40 minutes** / Servings: **4**

6 to 8 ounces pork tenderloin, trimmed of silver skin, halved lengthwise, cut into ¼-inch slices

¼ cup soy sauce

14-ounce container firm tofu, drained

One 4-by-6-inch piece kombu seaweed

4 medium dried shiitake mushrooms

3 small carrots, peeled and cut into ½-inch pieces

2-inch chunk daikon (about 5 ounces), peeled, cut into ½-inch pieces

3 scallions, thinly sliced on diagonal, white and green parts reserved separately

3 tablespoons sake

5 tablespoons white miso

Miso gives this simple soup—inspired by a recipe from Japanese cooking expert Elizabeth Andoh—great depth of flavor and a unique savoriness. Of the various types of miso, we liked the mild, subtle sweetness of white (shiro) miso best in this dish, but use any variety you like. For more complexity, you can even blend several different ones.

Don't allow the kombu-shiitake broth to reach a full boil. High heat damages the kombu's delicate flavors and will result in a pungent, overpowering broth.

1. In a small bowl, stir together the pork and soy sauce. Cover and refrigerate for at least 20 minutes or up to 1 hour. Meanwhile, line a baking dish with a triple layer of paper towels. Set the tofu in it and cover with additional paper towels. Place a second baking dish or plate on top, then weigh it down with several cans. Let stand for 10 minutes, then discard any accumulated liquid. Pat the tofu dry, cut it into ½-inch cubes and set aside.

2. Meanwhile, in a large saucepan over medium-high, bring 5 cups water, the kombu and mushrooms to a simmer; do not boil. Reduce to medium-low and cook, adjusting the heat to maintain a gentle simmer, for about 15 minutes, skimming off any small particles or foam on the surface.

3. Remove and discard the kombu and mushrooms. Add the tofu, carrots, daikon, scallion whites and sake. Bring to a gentle simmer over medium and cook until the vegetables are tender, 5 to 9 minutes.

4. Pour off and discard the excess pork marinade, then stir the pork into the soup. Cook until the pork is no longer pink, about 2 minutes. In a small bowl, whisk the miso and ¼ cup of the hot broth until dissolved, then stir into the soup. Ladle into bowls and sprinkle with scallion greens.

Taiwanese Beef Noodle Soup

Start to finish: 2 hours 45 minutes (45 minutes active) / Servings: 6

1 tablespoon grapeseed
or other neutral oil

6 medium garlic cloves, smashed
and peeled

4-inch piece fresh ginger, peeled,
cut into 6 to 8 pieces and smashed

6 scallions, white parts roughly
chopped, green parts thinly sliced,
reserved separately

3 star anise pods

1 tablespoon Sichuan peppercorns

3 tablespoons chili bean sauce (toban
djan, see note)

2 tablespoons tomato paste

2 tablespoons packed dark
brown sugar

⅓ cup soy sauce

⅓ cup sake

2 to 2½ pounds beef shanks
(about 1 inch thick), trimmed

Kosher salt

1 pound baby bok choy, trimmed
and cut crosswise into 1-inch pieces

8 ounces dried wheat noodles

Fragrant star anise and Sichuan peppercorns flavor this meaty broth, along with toban djan, a spicy, fermented chili-bean paste. It's sold in most Asian markets, but if you can't find it, substitute with 2 tablespoons white miso mixed with 4 teaspoons chili-garlic sauce and 2 teaspoons soy sauce. The soup is lightly spicy; you can add more toban djan and/or some ground Sichuan pepper at the table for more heat and spice. Chinese wheat noodles of any thickness worked well, as did Japanese udon and long, thin Italian pastas, such as spaghetti.

Don't forget to skim the fat off the strained cooking liquid. This prevents the soup from tasting greasy. And don't rinse the drained noodles under cold water. Lukewarm water will keep them from cooling down completely.

1. In a large Dutch oven over medium, combine the oil, garlic, ginger and scallion whites. Cook, stirring, until sizzling, about 3 minutes. Stir in the star anise and peppercorns, then cook until fragrant, about 30 seconds. Stir in the chili-bean sauce, tomato paste, brown sugar, soy sauce, sake and 2½ cups water. Bring to a boil over high.

2. Add the beef shanks and return to a simmer. Cover, reduce to low and cook, adjusting as needed to maintain a gentle simmer, until the beef is tender and beginning to fall apart, about 2 hours.

3. Use a slotted spoon to transfer the beef shanks to a bowl and set aside. Pour the cooking liquid through a fine mesh strainer set over a large bowl; discard the solids. Reserve the pot. Skim off and discard the fat from the surface

of the liquid, then return to the pot. When cool enough to handle, shred the meat into bite-size pieces, discarding the bones, fat and gristle. Add the meat to the pot and bring to a simmer over medium-high, then reduce to low and cover to keep warm.

4. In a large pot, bring 4 quarts water to a boil. Add 2 tablespoons salt and the bok choy. Cook until the stems are crisp-tender, about 3 minutes. Use a slotted spoon to transfer the bok choy to a large plate and set aside. Add the noodles to the water and cook until tender. Drain, rinse under lukewarm water, then drain again.

5. Divide the noodles and bok choy among serving bowls, then ladle in the soup and sprinkle with scallion greens.

Georgian Chicken Soup (*Chikhirtma*)

Start to finish: 1 hour 45 minutes (45 minutes active) / Servings: 6

For the broth and chicken:

1 bunch fresh cilantro

1 bunch fresh dill

1 garlic head

2½ to 3 pounds bone-in skin-on chicken legs

10 cups water

1 large yellow onion, quartered

2 teaspoons kosher salt

1 teaspoon black peppercorns

½ teaspoon coriander seeds

½ teaspoon red pepper flakes (optional)

3-inch cinnamon stick

2 bay leaves

For the soup:

1 pound carrots (about 5 medium), peeled, halved lengthwise and cut crosswise into ½-inch pieces

1 large yellow onion, coarsely chopped

3 tablespoons salted butter

½ teaspoon kosher salt

½ cup dry vermouth

1 tablespoon all-purpose flour

6 large egg yolks

¼ cup lemon juice

Ground black pepper

It's easy to overcomplicate chicken soup. Too often, the broths are watery and flavorless, so we compensate by piling on the ingredients. But that only leads to a muddle of flavors and textures. We wanted a chicken soup that tastes fresh and light, yet also robust and satisfying. We wanted just the right vegetables—and in the right volumes—balanced by a gentle acidity and spice. We found our answer in chikhirtma, a traditional soup from Georgia, the Eurasian country that bridges Turkey and Russia. Georgian cuisine often marries Western techniques with Eastern flavors. We used a recipe from Darra Goldstein, author of "The Georgian Feast," as our starting point. Her chikhirtma calls for a whole chicken, but that much meat made the soup feel heavy, so we used just chicken legs. We built flavor with bunches of dill and cilantro stems and a head of garlic, as well as coriander, cinnamon and bay leaves.

Don't simmer the soup after adding the eggs. Heat it gently just until warm, otherwise the eggs will curdle.

1. To make the broth, tie the stems of the cilantro and dill into bundles, then trim off the leaves, reserving ¼ cup of each for garnish. Cut off and discard the top third of the garlic head, leaving the head intact. In a large pot, combine both sets of stems, the garlic, the chicken and the remaining broth ingredients. Bring to a boil, then reduce heat to medium-low. Simmer until chicken is tender, about 45 minutes. Remove and set aside the garlic head. Transfer the chicken to a plate and cool until easily handled. Shred the chicken into bite-size pieces, discarding the skin, bones and cartilage. Set aside.

2. To make the soup, strain the broth into another pot or bowl, discarding the solids. Using tongs, squeeze the garlic head into the broth; the tender cloves should easily pop out of their skins. Whisk into the broth. Wipe out the empty pot, then add the carrots, onion, butter and salt. Set over medium-high and cook, stirring occasionally, until the onion is browned, 10 to 12 minutes. Add the vermouth, scraping up any browned bits, and cook until evaporated, 1 to 2 minutes. Add the flour and cook, stirring constantly, for 1 minute. Add 2 cups of the broth and stir until smooth, then add the remaining broth and bring to a simmer.

3. In a medium bowl, whisk the yolks. Continue whisking while slowly adding 1 cup of hot broth from the pot. Whisk in the lemon juice, then return the mixture to the pot and whisk to combine. Add the chicken and any accumulated juices and cook until just heated through (do not simmer). Taste and season with salt and pepper. Serve with the reserved chopped cilantro and dill leaves.

Spicy Red Lentil Stew with Coconut Milk and Spinach

Start to finish: 1 hour (10 minutes active) / Servings: 4 to 6

---

1 medium yellow onion, chopped

2 tablespoons coconut
or peanut oil

4 garlic cloves, smashed and peeled

Kosher salt

3 teaspoons finely grated
fresh ginger, divided

2 teaspoons mustard seeds

2 teaspoons ground turmeric

1 teaspoon ground coriander

1 teaspoon ground fennel seeds

¾ teaspoon red pepper flakes

14-ounce can coconut milk

1 cup split red lentils, rinsed
and drained

6 ounces (about 6 cups)
baby spinach, roughly chopped

2 tablespoons lime juice

Unsweetened coconut flakes
and chopped tomato, to garnish
(optional)

Located on the southwestern coast of India, Goa is known for its use of chilies, spices, coconut and bright acid (an influence from Portuguese colonization). Our spicy red lentil soup is a simplified take on a Goan staple that delivers a complete vegetarian meal in about an hour. Split red lentils, the foundation of the dish, cook in minutes. Blending turmeric, coriander and fennel created complex flavor. Fresh ginger brought welcome brightness, and adding a portion of it at the end kept the flavor vibrant. Both virgin and refined coconut oil worked, but virgin had a slightly stronger flavor. Mustard seeds added a peppery pop to the dish.

Don't substitute brown or green lentils for the split red lentils. Red lentils break down as they cook, thickening the cooking liquid and providing the ideal texture for the soup. Other lentil varieties remain intact even when fully cooked.

1. In a large saucepan over medium-high, combine the onion, oil, garlic and 1½ teaspoons of salt. Cook, stirring occasionally, until the onions have softened and are just beginning to color, 7 to 9 minutes. Stir in 2 teaspoons of ginger, the mustard seeds, turmeric, coriander, fennel and pepper flakes. Cook, stirring frequently, until fragrant, about 1 minute. Add 3½ cups water, coconut milk and lentils, then bring to a boil. Reduce heat to low, cover and cook until the lentils have broken down, 30 to 40 minutes.

2. Stir in the spinach and return to a simmer. Off the heat, add the remaining 1 teaspoon of ginger and the lime juice. Season with salt. Serve, garnished with coconut flakes and tomato, if using.

Mexican Chicken Soup
with Tomatillos and Hominy

Start to finish: 2 hours (1 hour active) / Servings: 6

---

2 large white onions,
1 quartered and 1 chopped

1 bunch fresh cilantro, stems
and leaves separated

2 whole dried ancho or pasilla
chilies, stemmed, seeded and
torn into rough pieces

2 tablespoons coriander seeds,
toasted, plus 1 tablespoon ground
coriander

2 tablespoons cumin seeds,
toasted, plus 1 tablespoon
ground cumin

Kosher salt

1 head of garlic

2½ to 3 pounds bone-in
skin-on chicken legs

2 fresh poblano chilies

2 fresh jalapeño chilies

1 pound fresh tomatillos,
husked and quartered

2 tablespoons grapeseed
or other neutral oil

2 teaspoons dried oregano,
preferably Mexican

15-ounce can hominy, drained

Toasted pepitas, lime wedges and
sour cream or Mexican crema
(optional), to serve

For a fresh take on chicken soup we looked to Mexico for inspiration and came up with one that builds layer upon layer of flavor—spice, chilies and herbs. We used charred fresh jalapeño and poblano peppers, a flavor-boosting technique common to Mexican and Latin American cooking. For our dried spices we added depth with relatively little effort by using toasted whole as well as ground coriander and cumin. Bone-in, skin-on chicken legs gave us broth-thickening collagen. For more spice, use serranos instead of jalapeños, or include the chilies' seeds. If you can't find fresh tomatillos, substitute canned tomatillos, drained. The broth and chicken can be made a day ahead and refrigerated separately before proceeding. However, shred the chicken while it's still warm. We liked garnishing the soup with chopped avocado, sliced jalapeños, crumbled queso fresco and fried tortilla strips.

Don't leave out the tomatillos. They give the soup acidity and texture.

1. In a large pot, combine 10 cups water, the quartered onion, cilantro stems, dried chilies, coriander seeds, cumin seeds and 1 teaspoon salt. Cut off and discard the top third of the garlic head, leaving the head intact, and add to the pot. Cover and bring to a boil, then simmer for 10 minutes. Add the chicken and return to a boil. Reduce heat to medium-low and cook partially covered for 30 minutes, maintaining a gentle simmer.

2. Meanwhile, heat the broiler to high with an oven rack 6 inches from the element. Arrange the poblanos and jalapeños on a rimmed baking sheet and broil, turning frequently, until evenly blackened and blistered, 10 to 12 minutes. Transfer to a bowl, cover tightly and set aside. Chop the cilantro leaves and set aside.

3. Peel, stem and seed the charred chilies, then roughly chop and add to a food processor along with the tomatillos. Pulse until coarsely chopped, 6 to 8 pulses.

4. Transfer the chicken and garlic head to a plate and let cool. Strain the broth, discarding the solids. Wipe out the pot. Add the oil, chopped onion and ½ teaspoon salt. Cook over medium-high, stirring occasionally, until softened and beginning to brown, 7 to 9 minutes. Add the ground coriander, ground cumin and oregano and cook, stirring constantly, for 1 minute. Add the tomatillo-chili mixture and cook, stirring frequently and scraping up any browned bits, until most of the moisture has evaporated, about 5 minutes. Add the broth and bring to a boil.

5. Shred the chicken into bite-size pieces, discarding the skin, bones and cartilage. Using tongs, squeeze the garlic head into the soup. The tender cloves should easily pop out of their skins. Add the chicken and hominy. Return to a simmer and cook until heated through, about 5 minutes. Stir in ½ cup of the chopped cilantro, then taste and season with salt. Top the soup with toasted pepitas, lime juice, more chopped cilantro and sour cream, if desired.

Vietnamese Meatball and Watercress Soup (*Canh*)

Start to finish: 40 minutes / Servings: 4

1 pound ground pork

6 scallions, white parts finely chopped, green parts thinly sliced, reserved separately

1 large egg white, lightly beaten

3 tablespoons fish sauce, divided

4 teaspoons finely grated fresh ginger, divided

Kosher salt and ground white pepper

2 tablespoons grapeseed or other neutral oil

1 medium yellow onion, chopped

4 medium garlic cloves, thinly sliced

2 quarts low-sodium chicken broth or water

1 bunch watercress, cut into 1½-inch lengths (4 cups lightly packed)

2 tablespoons lime juice

This refreshing supper is a take on canh, a type of quick, brothy Vietnamese soup. The soups (pronounced KUN) can be sour, rich with vegetables, or loaded with seafood. But whatever variety, the unifying factor is simplicity. Our version stays true to the simplicity, but scales up the ingredients so it can serve as a satisfying meal on its own. Watercress adds a peppery note; look for "live" watercress, which is packaged with its roots attached. It stays fresher longer and is easier to clean. To prep it, trim off and discard the roots, rinse and drain the greens, then cut them into 1½-inch lengths, discarding any stems that are thick or tough. If you prefer, substitute an equal amount of baby spinach for the watercress, but roughly chop the leaves before using. We also liked this soup made with chicken bouillon paste instead of chicken broth; use 2 tablespoons of paste dissolved in 2 quarts of water.

Don't leave the meatballs at room temperature after shaping them. Chilling firms them so they hold together in the simmering broth.

1. Line a rimmed baking sheet with kitchen parchment and mist with cooking spray. In a medium bowl, combine the pork, scallion whites, egg white, 1 tablespoon of fish sauce, 2 teaspoons of ginger, 1¼ teaspoons salt and 1 teaspoon white pepper. Mix with your hands. Lightly moisten your hands with water and form into 20 balls, each about a generous tablespoon. Set on the prepared baking sheet, cover and refrigerate.

2. In a large Dutch oven over medium, heat the oil until shimmering. Add the onion and cook, stirring, until beginning to soften, about 5 minutes. Stir in the remaining 2 teaspoons ginger and the garlic, then cook until fragrant, about

30 seconds. Add the broth and bring to a boil over high. Reduce to medium-low and simmer, uncovered, until the onion is fully softened, about 10 minutes.

3. Add the meatballs, then bring to a simmer over medium-high. Reduce the heat to maintain a gentle simmer and cook without stirring until the meatballs are cooked through, 8 to 10 minutes; they should reach 160°F at the center.

4. Off heat, stir in the watercress and the remaining 2 tablespoons fish sauce. Let stand until the greens are wilted and tender, about 1 minute. Stir in the lime juice. Taste and season with salt and pepper, then stir in the scallion greens.

Black-Eyed Pea and Sweet Potato Stew (*Ndambe*)

Start to finish: **40 minutes** / Servings: **6**

2 tablespoons unrefined coconut oil

1 large yellow onion, finely chopped

Kosher salt and ground black pepper

8 medium garlic cloves, minced

2 Fresno chilies, stemmed and sliced into thin rings

Three 14½-ounce cans black-eyed peas, rinsed and drained

2 bay leaves

1 pound sweet potatoes, peeled and cut into ½-inch cubes

1 pound plum tomatoes, cored and chopped

1 cup finely chopped fresh flat-leaf parsley

2 tablespoons lemon juice, plus lemon wedges, to serve

Both sweet potatoes and black-eyed peas are staples of West African cooking. In this recipe for Senegalese ndambe (pronounced NAM-bay), they're simmered together to make a hearty vegetarian stew. Canned black-eyed peas keep this dish fast and simple.

Don't use neutral-flavored oil in place of the coconut oil. Coconut oil—particularly unrefined—infuses the stew with a sweet flavor while adding richness.

1. In a large Dutch oven over medium, heat the coconut oil until shimmering. Add the onion, 2 teaspoons salt and ½ teaspoon pepper, then cook, stirring, until the onion is light golden brown and softened, 7 to 10 minutes.

2. Stir in the garlic and chilies, then cook until fragrant, about 30 seconds. Add the black-eyed peas, bay leaves and 5 cups water. Bring to a simmer over medium-high, then reduce to medium and cook, uncovered, stirring occasionally, for about 15 minutes.

3. Stir in the sweet potatoes and 2 teaspoons salt. Cover, reduce to medium-low and cook until the potatoes are tender, 10 to 15 minutes. Off heat, stir in the tomatoes, parsley and lemon juice. Taste and season with salt and pepper. Serve with lemon wedges.

Spanish Garlic Soup

Start to finish: 45 minutes / Servings: 4

6 scallions, trimmed and thinly sliced, whites and greens divided

6 medium garlic cloves, thinly sliced

6 tablespoons extra-virgin olive oil, divided, plus extra

4 teaspoons sweet paprika

1½ teaspoons smoked paprika

6 ounces sourdough or other rustic bread, cut into ½-inch cubes (about 4 cups), divided

2 tablespoons chicken bouillon

Kosher salt and ground black pepper

4 large egg yolks

Sherry vinegar, to taste

José Andrés taught us this "end of month" recipe—the sort of meal to make quickly with whatever is on hand and when money is tight. His approach: garlic cooked in copious amounts of olive oil with handfuls of thinly sliced stale bread and several tablespoons of smoked paprika. Add some water and simmer, then off heat stir in four or five whisked eggs. Supper is served. For our version, we realized the leftover bread, garlic and smoked paprika we had in our cupboards weren't up to Andrés' standards. So we needed to tweak. We boosted flavor by using chicken bouillon (an easy pantry flavor enhancer) instead of plain water, and we sautéed both sweet and smoked paprika with garlic and scallions. We actually didn't have stale bread, so we turned a loaf of rustic sourdough (a baguette or any crusty loaf will do) into delicious croutons, and added a bit of bread directly to the broth to thicken it. To serve, the soup and croutons are married in the serving bowls, allowing each person to adjust the ratio of soup to bread, as well as how long they soak.

Don't skip tempering the egg yolks with some of the hot broth before adding to the soup. This prevents them from curdling in the hot broth.

1. In a medium saucepan over medium-low, combine the scallion whites, garlic and 3 tablespoons of the oil. Cook, stirring occasionally, until beginning to color, 8 to 10 minutes. Add both paprikas and cook, stirring, until fragrant and darkened, 30 seconds.

2. Add 1 cup of the bread cubes and stir well. Whisk in 6 cups water and bouillon, increase heat to medium-high and bring to a simmer. Reduce heat to medium-low and simmer, whisking occasionally, for 15 minutes. Whisk vigorously to ensure bread is thoroughly broken up.

3. Meanwhile, in a 12-inch skillet over medium, combine the remaining 3 tablespoons of oil, the remaining 3 cups of bread, the scallion greens and ½ teaspoon each salt and pepper. Cook, stirring occasionally, until browned and crisp, 8 to 10 minutes.

4. In a medium bowl, whisk the egg yolks. Slowly whisk in 1 cup of the hot broth. Remove the soup from the heat. Off heat, vigorously whisk the egg yolks into the soup, then whisk in the vinegar. Taste and season with salt and pepper. To serve, fill individual bowls with the crouton mixture, then ladle the soup over them. Drizzle with additional oil, if desired.

Senegalese Braised Chicken with Onions and Lime (*Yassa Ginaar*)

Start to finish: 1 hour 15 minutes, plus marinating / Servings: 4

4 tablespoons peanut oil, divided

3 tablespoons grated lime zest, plus 6 tablespoons lime juice

1 habañero chili, seeded and minced

Kosher salt and ground black pepper

2 teaspoons chicken bouillon concentrate (see note)

2 pounds bone-in, skin-on chicken breasts, thighs or drumsticks, trimmed

3 medium yellow onions, halved and thinly sliced

Finely chopped fresh chives, to serve

With just a few ingredients, yassa ginaar delivers multiple layers of flavor—savory yet sweet with lightly caramelized onions, citrusy with lime zest and juice, meaty from deeply browned chicken, and spicy from the heat of a habañero chili. Our version is based on a recipe in "Yolele!" by Pierre Thiam, who marinates and sears the chicken, then uses the marinade as a base for the flavorful sauce. Bouillon concentrate adds to the savoriness of the dish; our preferred brand is Better than Bouillon. Serve with steamed rice.

Don't marinate the chicken for longer than two hours; the acidity of the lime juice will soften the meat. Don't use an uncoated cast-iron pot to cook this dish. The lime's acidity will react with the metal, causing the sauce to taste metallic.

1. In a large bowl, stir together 3 tablespoons of oil, the lime zest, habañero, 1 tablespoon salt and 1 teaspoon pepper. Transfer 2 teaspoons of the mixture to a small bowl and set aside. To the remaining oil-zest mixture, whisk in the lime juice, bouillon concentrate and ¼ cup water. Add the chicken and onions and toss. Cover and marinate at room temperature for 1 hour or refrigerate up to 2 hours, stirring once.

2. Remove the chicken from the marinade and pat dry with paper towels. Set a colander over a large bowl and drain the onions, reserving both the marinade and the onions.

3. In a large Dutch oven over medium-high, heat the remaining 1 tablespoon oil until barely smoking. Add the chicken, skin side down, and cook until well browned, about 4 minutes. Transfer to a plate and pour off and discard all but

1 tablespoon of the fat. Set the pot over medium heat and stir in the onions and ¼ cup water, scraping up any browned bits. Cover and cook, stirring frequently, until the onions are softened and lightly browned, 15 to 20 minutes.

4. Stir the reserved marinade into the onions. Return the chicken, skin side up, to the pot, nestling the pieces in the onions, then pour in any accumulated juices. Reduce to medium-low, cover and cook, stirring occasionally, until a skewer inserted into the thickest part of the meat meets no resistance, about 25 minutes.

5. Using a slotted spoon, transfer the chicken to a serving platter or shallow bowl. Off heat, stir the reserved oil-zest mixture into the onions, then taste and season with salt and pepper. Spoon the onions and sauce around the chicken and sprinkle with chives.

Thai Rice Soup (*Khao Tom*)

Start to finish: **35 minutes** / Servings: 4

---

8 ounces ground pork

3 tablespoons fish sauce, divided, plus extra to serve

2 tablespoons chili-garlic sauce, divided, plus extra to serve

Ground white pepper

3 tablespoons lard or refined coconut oil

5 large shallots, peeled, halved lengthwise and thinly sliced (2 cups)

Kosher salt

8 medium garlic cloves, thinly sliced

3 lemon grass stalks, trimmed to bottom 6 inches, dry outer leaves removed, smashed

2 tablespoons finely grated fresh ginger

2½ quarts low-sodium chicken broth

4 cups cooked and chilled jasmine rice (see note)

1 cup chopped fresh cilantro

3 tablespoons lime juice, plus lime wedges, to serve

Fried shallots, to serve (see recipe)

Soft- or hard-cooked eggs, peeled and halved, to serve

Savory pork meatballs and jasmine rice give this Thai soup heft, but its aromatic broth—made with plenty of shallots, garlic, lemon grass and ginger—has excellent flavor on its own. The soup is a sort of blank canvas for garnishes; the recipe calls for our favorites, but feel free to offer only those that appeal to you.

Don't use freshly cooked rice, as the grains will turn mushy. Rice that was cooked at least a day in advance, then chilled, held its shape better than rice that was cooked the same day. To chill just-cooked rice, mist a parchment-lined baking sheet with cooking spray and spread the hot rice on it evenly. Let cool to room temperature, cover and refrigerate for at least four hours or up to three days.

1. In a medium bowl, combine the pork, 1 tablespoon of fish sauce, 1 tablespoon of chili-garlic sauce and ¾ teaspoon white pepper. Mix with your hands. Form the mixture into 20 meatballs (about 2 teaspoons each), rolling each between the palms of your hands. Place on a large plate.

2. In a large Dutch oven over medium-high, heat the lard until shimmering. Add the shallots and ½ teaspoon salt and cook, stirring occasionally, until browned, about 5 minutes. Stir in the garlic and cook until fragrant, about 30 seconds. Stir in the lemon grass and ginger and cook until fragrant, about 30 seconds. Add the broth and bring to a boil, scraping up any browned bits, then reduce to medium and simmer uncovered for about 15 minutes.

3. Remove and discard the lemon grass. Add the meatballs, stir gently to combine and simmer over medium until the meatballs are just cooked through, 3 to 4 minutes. Stir in the rice and cook until heated through, about 1 minute. Off heat, stir in the remaining 2 tablespoons fish sauce, the remaining 1 tablespoon chili-garlic sauce, 1 teaspoon white pepper, the cilantro and lime juice. Ladle into bowls and serve with fried shallots, egg halves, chili-garlic sauce and lime wedges.

FRIED SHALLOTS

A mandoline works well for slicing the shallots, but a sharp knife does the job, too. Fried shallots are a great garnish on soups, salads, fried rice and noodle dishes. The oil left over from frying the shallots is infused with flavor; use it for stir-frying, sautéing and in salad dressings.

Don't be tempted to turn the heat up once the shallots are added to the oil. Moderate heat and frequent stirring ensure the shallots brown evenly and without scorching.

Start to finish: 20 minutes
Makes about 1½ cups

1 cup grapeseed or other neutral oil

12 ounces shallots, thinly sliced

1. Line a large plate with a triple layer of paper towels. Place a mesh strainer over a heat-safe medium bowl and set near the stove.

2. In a large saucepan over medium-high, heat the oil to about 275°F; a slice of shallot dropped in the oil should sizzle immediately. Add the shallots and reduce to medium. Cook, stirring, until golden brown, 8 to 10 minutes. Drain immediately in the strainer and shake the strainer to remove excess oil.

3. Using tongs, transfer the shallots to the prepared plate, spreading them in an even layer. Let cool completely. Store the shallots and oil separately in airtight containers. The shallots will keep for up to 1 week at room temperature; the oil will keep for up to 1 month in the refrigerator.

Somali Chicken Soup

Start to finish: 50 minutes / Servings: 6

---

1 tablespoon grapeseed or other neutral oil

2 large yellow onions, chopped

Kosher salt and ground white pepper

2 serrano chilies, stemmed and sliced into thin rounds

4 medium garlic cloves, smashed and peeled

4 teaspoons ground coriander

2 teaspoons ground cardamom

1 bunch fresh cilantro, stems chopped, leaves finely chopped, reserved separately

4 plum tomatoes, cored, seeded and chopped, divided

1½ quarts low-sodium chicken broth or water

Four 12-ounce bone-in, skin-on chicken breasts

1½ cups jasmine or basmati rice, rinsed and drained

2 tablespoons lime juice, plus lime wedges, to serve

Thinly sliced radishes and/or chopped red cabbage, to serve (optional)

Green chili sauce, berbere sauce or other hot sauce, to serve (see recipes p. 71)

Serve this soup family style: Bring the pot to the table along with the radishes, cabbage and lime wedges, then have diners fill and garnish their bowls as they like. Offer a simple homemade or store-bought hot sauce alongside. Hot steamed rice, added to bowls before the soup is ladled in, is a satisfying addition.

Don't use boneless, skinless chicken breasts. Both the bones and skin contribute flavor to the broth.

1. In a large Dutch oven over medium, heat the oil until shimmering. Add the onions and ½ teaspoon salt and cook, stirring, until beginning to brown, about 5 minutes. Add the chilies, garlic, coriander, cardamom, cilantro stems and half of the tomatoes. Cook, stirring constantly, until fragrant, about 30 seconds.

2. Add the broth and bring to a simmer over high. Submerge the chicken breasts in the broth, cover and cook over low until a skewer inserted in the thickest part of the chicken meets no resistance or the chicken reaches 160°F, about 30 minutes.

3. Meanwhile, in a medium saucepan, combine the rice, 2 cups water and 1 teaspoon salt. Bring to a simmer over medium-high, then reduce to low and cook, covered, until the liquid is absorbed and the rice is tender, 15 to 20 minutes. Off heat, remove the lid, lay a clean dish towel over the pot, replace the cover and let stand for about 10 minutes or until ready to serve.

4. Using tongs, transfer the chicken to a large plate and set aside to cool. Pour the broth through a fine mesh strainer set over a large heatproof bowl; discard the solids. Return the broth to the pot. When the chicken is cool enough to handle, shred the meat into bite-size pieces, discarding the skin and bones.

5. Add the chicken to the broth and bring to a simmer over medium-high. Remove from the heat and stir in the remaining tomatoes, the cilantro leaves and lime juice. Taste and season with salt and pepper.

6. To serve, fluff the rice with a fork, then mound a portion into each serving bowl. Ladle the soup over the rice, then top each portion with radishes and/or cabbage (if using) and the hot sauces. Serve with lime wedges.

GREEN CHILI SAUCE

This sauce is spicy and sharp on its own, but a spoonful stirred into a serving of soup provides the perfect flavor accent. Refrigerate leftovers in an airtight container for up to a week.

Start to finish: **5 minutes**
Makes about **1 cup**

1 plum tomato, cored and quartered

5 serrano chilies, stemmed

3 tablespoons lime juice

2 medium garlic cloves, smashed and peeled

1½ teaspoons kosher salt

In a blender, combine all ingredients and process until smooth, 1 to 2 minutes, scraping the sides as needed.

BERBERE SAUCE

For this bold, paste-like sauce, macerating the onion in lime juice tempers its harsh bite. For a brighter flavor, substitute sweet paprika instead of smoked. This sauce is best used the day it is made.

Start to finish: **15 minutes**
Makes about: **¼ cup**

3 tablespoons lime juice

1 tablespoon minced red onion

½ teaspoon kosher salt

1 tablespoon smoked paprika

1 teaspoon ground coriander

1 teaspoon ground ginger

½ teaspoon cayenne pepper

¼ teaspoon ground cardamom

1. In a small bowl, stir together the lime juice, onion and salt. Let stand for 10 minutes.

2. Meanwhile, in a small skillet over medium-low, toast the paprika, coriander, ginger, cayenne and cardamom, stirring constantly, until fragrant, 1 to 2 minutes. Remove from the heat and let cool for 10 minutes. Stir the spices into the lime juice-onion mixture.

Vegetables

4

Avocado Salad with Pickled Mustard Seeds and Marjoram Vinaigrette

Start to finish: **1 hour** / Servings: **6**

For the pickled mustard seeds:

¼ cup yellow mustard seeds

½ cup cider vinegar

¼ cup white sugar

¼ cup water

1½ teaspoons black peppercorns

½ teaspoon coriander seeds

3 allspice berries

1 bay leaf

⅛ teaspoon red pepper flakes

For the dressing:

2 tablespoons pickled mustard seeds and brine

1 tablespoon minced shallot

2 teaspoons whole-grain mustard

1 teaspoon honey

¼ teaspoon kosher salt

¼ teaspoon ground black pepper

¼ cup chopped fresh marjoram

3 tablespoons canola oil

3 tablespoons extra-virgin olive oil

For the salad:

3 firm but ripe avocados

Kosher salt

6 teaspoons lemon juice

Thinly sliced ricotta salata cheese

Fresh marjoram leaves

It was the simplicity that we loved. Half an avocado, sliced and fanned across a plate. Over it, marjoram vinaigrette studded with tender spheres of pickled mustard seeds. One thing was quite clear: A handful of simple ingredients can take a stunning turn when the right flavors tie them together. In this case, that is the role of the whole mustard seeds, an ingredient Americans rarely encounter outside pickle brine. We discovered this at Stephen Oxaal's Branch Line restaurant in Watertown, Massachusetts, where the seeds take an avocado salad from simple to stunning. The pickling process takes just a few minutes and the result adds a tang and crunch that balance the lushness of the other ingredients. Conventional vinaigrettes—blends of fat and acid—tended to slide off the avocados. Instead, we eliminated the lemon juice from the dressing and drizzled it directly over the avocado slices, where it mingled with the dressing. We liked ricotta salata best, but Parmesan was a fine substitute.

1. To make the pickled mustard seeds, in a small saucepan over high, combine the mustard seeds and enough water to cover by 2 inches. Bring to a boil, then reduce heat to medium-low and simmer until the seeds are tender, about 8 minutes. Strain the seeds through a mesh strainer and transfer to a bowl. Wipe out and reserve the pan.

2. To the pan, add the remaining pickling ingredients. Place over high heat. Bring to a boil, then reduce to medium-low and simmer until fragrant and the sugar has dissolved, 3 to 5 minutes. Strain over the mustard seeds, discarding the solids. Let the mixture cool to room temperature. Use immediately or cover and refrigerate for up to 4 weeks.

3. To make the dressing, in a small bowl, mix together 2 tablespoons of the pickled mustard seeds and brine, the shallot, mustard, honey, salt and pepper. Let sit for 10 minutes. Add the marjoram and both oils and whisk until emulsified.

4. To assemble and serve, halve the avocados lengthwise, remove the pits and peel away the skins. Cut each half into slices (see sidebar), leaving the halves intact, and fan onto serving plates, cut sides down. Sprinkle a pinch of salt and 1 teaspoon of lemon juice over each half. Spoon the dressing over the avocados and garnish with ricotta salata and marjoram.

HOW TO FAN AN AVOCADO

1. Halve each avocado lengthwise and remove the pit. Peel the skin from each half.

2. Place the avocado halves cut side down. Starting at the larger end of each half, cut each into 6 lengthwise slices, leaving the top 1 inch intact.

3. Set each half on a plate, cut side down. Gently press the large end to fan the slices.

Lebanese-Style **Tabbouleh**

Start to finish: **15 minutes** / Servings: 4

½ cup boiling water

⅓ cup fine-grain bulgur

1 teaspoon ground sumac (optional)

½ teaspoon ground allspice

Kosher salt and ground black pepper

3 tablespoons lemon juice

1 small shallot, minced

¼ teaspoon white sugar

¼ cup extra-virgin olive oil

2 to 3 small vine-ripened tomatoes, diced

4 cups lightly packed flat-leaf parsley leaves, well dried then minced

1 cup lightly packed mint leaves, well dried then minced

Israeli-born British chef Yotam Ottolenghi is clear about tabbouleh. It should be "all about the parsley." But in the U.S., the Middle Eastern salad often goes heavy on the bulgur, a wheat that has been cooked, dried and cracked. The result is a salad that is mealy, bland and stubbornly soggy. That's because the bulgur sponges up all the juices from the tomatoes. Our solution was to barely cook the bulgur—essentially underhydrating it—allowing it to soak up those juices without becoming waterlogged. We added generous helpings of herbs, livening up the parsley with some mint. Wet herbs will dilute the dressing and make the bulgur gummy. Be sure to dry them thoroughly with a spinner and paper towels before mincing. Some type of onion is traditional; we used shallots, preferring their gentler bite, and soaked them in lemon juice to soften their flavor and texture. While the sumac is optional, we loved its fruity complexity and light acidity.

Don't use coarse-grain bulgur; it won't hydrate evenly. If you can't find fine-grain bulgur, process medium- or coarse-grain in short pulses until fine, light and fluffy, five to 10 pulses.

1. In a medium bowl, combine the water, bulgur, sumac, if using, allspice and ½ teaspoon of salt. Cover with plastic wrap and let sit for 10 minutes. In a large bowl, stir together the lemon juice, shallot, sugar and ¾ teaspoon of salt; let sit for 10 minutes.

2. Whisk the oil into the lemon juice mixture. Fluff the bulgur with a fork and add to the dressing along with the tomatoes; mix well. Fold the parsley and mint into the tabbouleh, then taste and season with salt, pepper and additional sumac, if needed.

PARCH YOUR STARCH

Underhydrating starchy ingredients—such as pasta and bulgur—is a quick and easy way to boost the flavor of a dish. Underhydrated grains and pastas are able to absorb flavors from spices and sauces better, resulting in a more vibrant and appetizing dish.

We used this technique in our Lebanese-style tabbouleh, cutting back on the amount of water we normally would use to soak the bulgur, allowing it to better soak up the dressing and tomato juices without becoming watery.

Apple, Celery Root and Fennel Salad with Hazelnuts

Start to finish: **20 minutes** / Servings: 6

1 small shallot, grated

1½ tablespoons cider vinegar

3 tablespoons lightly packed grated fresh horseradish

3 tablespoons extra-virgin olive oil

1 teaspoon honey

Kosher salt and ground black pepper

1 Granny Smith apple, cored and cut into matchsticks

½ small celery root (about 8 ounces), peeled and cut into matchsticks

1 medium fennel bulb, trimmed and thinly sliced

½ cup chopped fresh parsley leaves

¼ cup chopped fresh mint leaves

½ cup hazelnuts, toasted and coarsely chopped

A winter salad needs to stand up to hearty stews and roasts, and that calls for bold, bright flavors. We started with tart apples and thin slices of fennel bulb, the latter adding a pleasant anise flavor. Celery root added a fresh crispness while grated fresh horseradish gave the dish kick. Grating the horseradish triggers a chemical reaction that enhances the root's bite. Tossing it with vinegar and salt helps preserve that heat, which otherwise dissipates quickly. Make sure you grate horseradish in an open and well-ventilated space.

Don't use prepared horseradish in this recipe. It's bottled with vinegar and salt that would alter the balance of flavors.

In a large bowl, combine the shallot and vinegar. Let sit for 10 minutes. Whisk in the horseradish, oil, honey, 1 teaspoon salt and ½ teaspoon pepper. Add the apple, celery root and fennel, then toss. Stir in the parsley and mint, then sprinkle with hazelnuts.

Thai-style Napa Coleslaw with Mint and Cilantro

Start to finish: 25 minutes / Servings: 6

---

3 tablespoons lime juice

4 teaspoons white sugar

1 tablespoon fish sauce

1 medium serrano chili, seeded and minced

5 tablespoons coconut milk

1 pound napa cabbage (1 small head), thinly sliced crosswise (about 8 cups)

6 radishes, trimmed, halved and thinly sliced

4 ounces sugar snap peas, strings removed, thinly sliced on diagonal

½ cup coarsely chopped fresh cilantro

½ cup coarsely chopped fresh mint

½ cup roasted, salted cashews, coarsely chopped

In rethinking the classic American coleslaw we took our inspiration from San Antonio chef Quealy Watson, whose slaw world changed when he traveled to Asia. Watson, the former chef at San Antonio's funky Tex-Asian barbecue joint Hot Joy, created a slaw inspired by traditional Burmese lahpet, fermented tea leaves that are eaten. For our slaw, we used tender napa cabbage with red radishes and snap peas for crunch, with fresh mint and cilantro to tie it all together. Coconut milk—instead of mayonnaise—had the right balance of richness and fresh flavor. For heat, we used a fresh chili "cooked" in lime juice, which mellowed the bite and helped disperse the heat evenly. Fish sauce added a savory pungency.

Don't use "light" coconut milk or sweetened "cream of coconut" for this recipe. The former is too thin, and the latter is too sweet (think pina coladas). And don't forget to vigorously shake the can before opening to ensure the fat and liquid are fully emulsified.

In a liquid measuring cup, mix together the lime juice, sugar, fish sauce and chili. Let sit for 10 minutes. Whisk in the coconut milk until combined, then adjust seasoning with additional fish sauce, if desired. In a large bowl, combine the cabbage, radishes, peas, cilantro and mint. Add the dressing and toss until evenly coated. Stir in the cashews and serve.

Kale Salad with Smoked Almonds and Picada Crumbs

Start to finish: **15 minutes** / Servings: 6

2 shallots, thinly sliced

5 tablespoons sherry vinegar

Kosher salt

2 tablespoons honey

8 tablespoons extra-virgin olive oil, divided

Ground black pepper

1 cup smoked almonds

4 ounces chewy white bread, cut into 1-inch cubes

2 teaspoons fresh thyme

1 tablespoon sweet paprika

2 bunches lacinato kale, stemmed, washed, spun dry and thinly sliced crosswise (10 cups)

1 cup lightly packed fresh mint, chopped

Kale can make a flavorful and seasonal winter salad, but to be eaten raw it needs to be treated right. Otherwise, the greens can be unpleasantly tough. We started with lacinato kale, also known as dinosaur or Tuscan kale. Its long blue-green leaves are sweeter and more tender than curly kale. Slicing the greens thinly was the first step to making them more salad-friendly. Then, to soften them further, we borrowed a Japanese technique used on raw cabbage—massaging the leaves. In this case, we do it with ground smoked almonds, which help tenderize the kale and add crunch and flavor to the finished salad. An acidic shallot-sherry vinaigrette also helped soften and brighten the kale (look for a sherry vinegar aged at least 3 years). Intensely flavorful paprika breadcrumbs, inspired by the Catalan sauce picada, tied everything together.

Don't slice the kale until you're ready to make the salad; it will wilt. You can, however, stem, wash and dry it ahead of time.

1. In a small bowl, whisk together the shallots, vinegar and ½ teaspoon salt. Let sit for 10 minutes. Whisk in the honey, 5 tablespoons of the oil and ½ teaspoon pepper; set aside.

2. In a food processor, process the almonds until coarsely chopped, about 8 pulses; transfer to a large bowl. Add the bread to the processor and process to rough crumbs, about 20 seconds. Add the thyme, the remaining 3 tablespoons oil, the paprika, ½ teaspoon salt and ½ teaspoon pepper. Process until incorporated, about 10 seconds.

3. Transfer the crumb mixture to a large skillet over medium and cook, stirring frequently, until crisp and browned, 8 to 10 minutes. Transfer to a plate to cool.

4. Add the kale and mint to the bowl with the almonds and massage the greens until the kale softens and darkens, 10 to 20 seconds. Add the dressing and crumbs and toss to combine. Taste, then season with salt and pepper.

Smashed Cucumber Salad

Start to finish: 40 minutes (15 minutes active) / Servings: 6

2 pounds English cucumbers
(about 2 large)

4 teaspoons white sugar

1 tablespoon kosher salt

4 teaspoons unseasoned
rice vinegar

1 medium garlic clove,
smashed and peeled

2 tablespoons grapeseed or
other neutral oil

½ teaspoon red pepper flakes

1½ tablespoons soy sauce

1 tablespoon toasted sesame oil

1 tablespoon grated fresh ginger

Cilantro leaves, sliced scallions
and toasted sesame seeds, to
serve (optional)

SALT YOUR WAY
TO CRISPER VEGETABLES

A toss with salt and sugar—followed
by a brief rest and draining—helps
remove excess water from vegetables. The science at work is osmosis,
the movement of water across a cell
membrane. In our smashed cucumber salad, the ruptured cells release
water. When we add sugar and salt,
they dissolve and make a concentrated solution outside the cucumber
cells. The solution acts like a magnet
to draw out water, thus helping to dry
the cucumbers.

Slick, watery vegetables such as sliced cucumbers can be hard to season;
dressings tend to slide right off. Yet across Asia there is a whole class
of boldly flavored salads made entirely of cucumber. What do they know
that we don't? Our answer came from China's pai huang gua, or smashed
cucumber salad. In this case, it's the prep work—not the dressing—that
sets the dish apart. The cucumbers are smashed, banged and whacked.
This works for two reasons. First, it ruptures more cell walls than slicing
and dicing, making it easier to remove the seeds, the main culprit in
watery cucumbers. Second, it creates craggy, porous surfaces that absorb
more dressing. The easiest way to smash cucumbers is to place a rolling
pin or the flat side of a chef's knife over them and smack it sharply with
your hand. To draw out even more moisture from the cucumbers, we
borrowed another Asian technique, salting and sugaring. In China, dressings vary by region. We blurred regional lines, combining garlic, soy sauce,
fresh ginger and pepper-infused oil.

*Don't substitute conventional, thick-sliced cucumbers for English. The ratio of
seeds to flesh is higher and the skins are too tough.*

1. Trim the ends off the cucumbers,
then halve lengthwise. Place each half
cut side down, then press a rolling pin or
the flat side of a broad knife against the
cucumber and hit firmly with the heel
of your hand. Repeat along the length of
the cucumbers until they crack. Pull the
sections apart, scraping and discarding
the seeds. Cut into rough ¾-inch pieces
and set in a large bowl.

2. In a small bowl, combine the sugar
and salt; toss the cucumbers with 5 teaspoons of the mixture. Transfer to a
colander set over a bowl. Refrigerate
for 30 to 60 minutes, tossing occasionally.
Meanwhile, stir the vinegar and garlic
into the remaining sugar-salt mixture.
Set aside.

3. In a small skillet over medium-low,
combine the grapeseed oil and pepper
flakes. Cook, stirring, until sizzling and
the pepper flakes begin to darken, 2 to
4 minutes. Strain the oil, discarding the
solids.

4. Remove and discard the garlic from
the vinegar mixture. Stir in the soy
sauce, sesame oil and ginger. Transfer
the drained cucumbers to a kitchen
towel and pat dry. In a bowl, stir together the cucumbers and dressing, then stir
in half of the chili oil. Serve drizzled with
more chili oil and sprinkled with cilantro,
scallions and sesame seeds, if desired.

French Carrot Salad

Start to finish: 20 minutes / Servings: 6

___

2 tablespoons white balsamic vinegar

2 tablespoons chopped fresh tarragon

1 tablespoon minced shallot

1 teaspoon honey

⅛ teaspoon cayenne pepper

Kosher salt

¼ cup extra-virgin olive oil

1¼ pounds carrots, peeled and shredded

1 cup chopped fresh parsley

Carrots tend to be a woody afterthought on U.S. salad bars. Here, we transform them into a lively side dish by taking a tip from France, where grated carrots stand alone as an iconic side dish—salade de carottes râpées. Grating fresh carrots releases their sugars and aromas, creating an earthy sweetness that just needs a bit of acid for balance. Using relatively mild white balsamic vinegar allowed us to up the vinegar-to-oil ratio (1:2) for a punchy but not overwhelming flavor. White balsamic also paired well with a touch of honey, which heightened the carrots' natural sweetness. The French have long favored handheld rotary graters to make this salad, but we found the food processor was the fastest and easiest way to shred carrots. We also liked the meatier shreds it produces, though a box grater works fine, too. No tarragon? Use 1½ teaspoons chopped fresh thyme instead.

Don't use old bagged carrots. This salad is all about the earthy, sweet carrot flavor. Large carrots can be woody, dry and bitter; small baby carrots are too juicy. Look for bunches of medium carrots with the greens still attached.

In a large bowl, whisk together the vinegar, tarragon, shallot, honey, cayenne and 1 teaspoon of salt. Let sit for 10 minutes. Whisk in the oil until emulsified, then add the carrots and parsley. Stir until evenly coated. Season with salt. Serve or refrigerate for up to 24 hours.

THE GRATEFUL SHRED

Grating root vegetables such as carrots makes them taste sweeter and fresher than chopping or slicing. That's because when the vegetable is cut, its cells rupture and release sugars and volatile hydrocarbons, the sources of the vegetable's sweetness and aroma. The more cells you rupture, the better the taste. And grating ruptures more cells than just about any other prep technique.

Grating also changes how the vegetables interact with dressing. The process creates a more porous surface on the pieces of vegetable and exposes more of that surface. Therefore, more dressing comes into contact with more vegetable. This allows the dressing to have an outsized effect on the finished dish.

Thai Stir-Fried Spinach

Start to finish: **20 minutes** / Servings: 4

1 tablespoon fish sauce

1 tablespoon oyster sauce

2 teaspoons white sugar

¾ teaspoon red pepper flakes

3 tablespoons grapeseed
or other neutral oil, divided

3 tablespoons roughly
chopped garlic

1½ pounds bunch spinach,
trimmed of bottom 1½ inches,
washed and dried

This simple, bold stir-fry uses regular bunch spinach rather than the water spinach common in Thai cooking. The wilted leaves and crisp-tender stems combine for a pleasing contrast of textures. Be sure to dry the spinach well after washing; excess water will cause splattering and popping when the spinach is added to the hot oil. A salad spinner works well, or roll the spinach in kitchen towels and squeeze dry. We liked to serve this with steamed jasmine rice to soak up the sauce.

Don't use baby spinach, which can't handle high-heat cooking and doesn't have stems to offer textural contrast. And don't allow the spinach leaves to fully wilt in the pan; some leaves should still look fairly fresh, but will continue to cook after being transferred to the bowl.

1. In a small bowl, whisk together the fish sauce, oyster sauce, sugar and pepper flakes until the sugar dissolves. Set aside.

2. In a 14-inch wok over medium-high, heat 2 tablespoons of the oil until barely smoking. Remove the wok from the heat, add the garlic and cook, stirring, until just beginning to color, 20 to 30 seconds. Return the wok to high and immediately add ½ of the spinach. Using tongs, turn the spinach to coat with the oil and garlic. When the spinach is nearly wilted and the garlic has turned golden brown, after 30 seconds or less, transfer to a large bowl. The leaves will continue to wilt but the stems should remain crisp-tender.

3. Return the wok to high heat. Add the remaining 1 tablespoon oil, swirl to coat the wok and heat until just beginning to smoke. Add the remaining spinach and cook as before, for 20 to 30 seconds. Transfer to the bowl with the first batch of spinach.

4. Pour the fish sauce mixture over the spinach and toss. Transfer to a platter and drizzle with any accumulated liquid.

Japanese Potato Salad

Start to finish: **1 hour (15 minutes active)** / Servings: 4

1 Persian cucumber, halved lengthwise and thinly sliced crosswise

1 medium carrot, peeled and shredded

¼ cup minced red onion

Kosher salt and ground black pepper

1½ pounds Yukon Gold potatoes, peeled and cut into ¾-inch pieces

3 tablespoons unseasoned rice vinegar

½ cup mayonnaise

2 ounces thick-cut smoked deli ham, diced (about ⅓ cup)

1 hard-cooked egg plus 1 hard-cooked egg yolk, diced

1 teaspoon white sugar

2 scallions, finely sliced

Getting potato salad right is no picnic. Too often the salad lacks the acidity or piquancy needed to cut through the richness of the mayonnaise. Our search for a better option led us to Japan, where potato salads are partially mashed to create a creamier texture. And they balance that texture with crumbled hard-boiled egg and the crisp bite of vegetables, such as cucumber and carrots. Tying everything together is Kewpie, a Japanese mayonnaise made with rice vinegar and egg yolks. It is smoother and richer than American mayonnaise. We started by looking for the right potatoes, which turned out to be Yukon Gold. Salting the cooking water ensured even seasoning, as did sprinkling them with vinegar and black pepper as they cooled. Waiting until the potatoes were at room temperature before adding mayonnaise was important to avoid oiliness. We used American mayonnaise but approximated the Kewpie flavor by increasing the vinegar and adding an extra hard-cooked egg yolk and 1 teaspoon of sugar. For a savory touch, we added diced ham and finished with scallions.

Don't substitute starchy russet or waxy new potatoes. The smooth texture of partly mashed Yukon Golds gave us the creamy consistency we wanted.

1. In a medium bowl, combine the cucumber, carrot, onion and 2 teaspoons of salt. Set aside. In a large saucepan over medium-high, combine the potatoes with enough water to cover by 1 inch. Add 1 teaspoon of salt and bring to a boil. Reduce heat to medium-high and simmer until tender, 12 to 15 minutes.

2. Drain the potatoes, then transfer to a large bowl. Using a fork, coarsely mash half of them. Sprinkle with the vinegar and ¾ teaspoon pepper. Stir to combine, then spread in an even layer along the bottom and sides of the bowl. Let cool for at least 20 minutes.

3. Transfer the vegetable mixture to a fine mesh strainer and rinse well. Working in batches, use your hands to squeeze the vegetables, removing as much liquid as possible, then add to the potatoes. Add the mayonnaise, ham, diced egg and yolk and sugar. Fold until thoroughly combined. Taste and season with salt and pepper, if necessary. Sprinkle with scallions, then serve chilled or at room temperature.

Fattoush

Start to finish: **30 minutes** / Servings: 6

1 pound seedless red grapes, halved

¼ cup cider vinegar

Kosher salt and ground black pepper

½ cup extra-virgin olive oil, divided

3 medium garlic cloves, finely grated

2 teaspoons ground cumin

½ to ¾ teaspoon red pepper flakes

Two 8-inch pita bread rounds, each
split into 2 rounds

½ cup plain whole-milk yogurt

½ cup finely chopped fresh dill

1 tablespoon pomegranate molasses
(optional)

2 teaspoons ground sumac (optional)

1 English cucumber, quartered
lengthwise, thinly sliced

6- to 7-ounce romaine heart,
chopped into bite-size pieces

1 cup lightly packed fresh mint,
finely chopped

This take on a Middle Eastern bread salad gets crunch and texture from pita bread split into rounds and brushed generously with seasoned olive oil before toasting to produce thin, crisp pieces packed with flavor. Pickled grapes are not a common fattoush ingredient, but we loved their sweet-tart flavor and succulent texture—they're an idea we borrowed from chef Ana Sortun of Oleana in Cambridge, Massachusetts. Both the pita and the grapes can be prepared a day in advance; store the pita in an airtight container to keep it fresh. Sumac, a fruity, lemony Levantine spice, has earthy, citrusy notes, and pomegranate molasses is tangy and lightly fruity. Both ingredients are optional, but they give the fattoush complexity and a distinct Middle Eastern character.

Don't combine the salad ingredients until just before serving or the pita chips will get soggy.

1. Heat the oven to 400°F with a rack in the middle position. In a medium bowl, stir together the grapes, vinegar and ½ teaspoon salt. Cover and refrigerate.

2. In a small bowl, stir together ¼ cup of oil, the garlic, cumin and pepper flakes. Arrange the pita rounds rough side up on a rimmed baking sheet, then brush each with the flavored oil, using all of it. Sprinkle with salt and black pepper. Bake until browned and crisp, 10 to 12 minutes. Set aside to cool. When cool enough to handle, break into bite-size pieces.

3. Drain the grapes, reserving the pickling liquid. In a large bowl, combine the remaining ¼ cup oil, the yogurt, dill, molasses and sumac, if using, and 1 teaspoon each of salt and pepper. Add the reserved pickling liquid and whisk well. Add the cucumber, romaine, mint, pickled grapes and pita pieces. Toss until evenly coated.

Shaved Zucchini and Herb Salad with Parmesan

Start to finish: **10 minutes** / Servings: 4

1 teaspoon grated lemon zest, plus 3 tablespoons juice

3 tablespoons extra-virgin olive oil

¼ teaspoon honey

Kosher salt and ground black pepper

1 pound zucchini (2 medium)

1 ounce Parmesan cheese, finely grated (about ½ cup), plus extra, shaved, to serve

½ cup lightly packed fresh mint, torn

½ cup lightly packed fresh basil, torn

¼ cup hazelnuts, toasted, skinned and coarsely chopped

For this vibrant salad, we adopted the Italian technique of slicing raw zucchini into thin ribbons. The zucchini really shines here, balanced with the clean, sharp flavors of lemon along with Parmesan and hazelnuts. A Y-style peeler makes it easy to shave the zucchini, or you can use a mandoline. Don't worry if the ribbons vary in width; this adds to the visual appeal of the dish. Toasted sliced, slivered or chopped whole almonds can be used in place of the hazelnuts.

Don't dress the salad until you are ready to serve. The zucchini and herbs are delicate and quickly wilt.

1. In a large bowl, whisk together the lemon zest and juice, oil, honey, ½ teaspoon salt and ¼ teaspoon pepper. Set aside.

2. Use a Y-style peeler or mandoline to shave the zucchini from top to bottom, rotating as you go. Stop shaving when you reach the seedy core. Discard the cores.

3. To the dressing, add the shaved zucchini, cheese, mint and basil. Gently toss until evenly coated. Transfer to a serving plate and sprinkle with shaved Parmesan and hazelnuts.

Bulgur-Tomato Salad with Herbs and Pomegranate Molasses (*Eetch*)

Start to finish: **30 minutes** / Servings: 4

3 tablespoons tomato paste

2 tablespoons extra-virgin olive oil

1 medium red bell pepper, stemmed, seeded and finely chopped

6 scallions (4 finely chopped, 2 thinly sliced, reserved separately)

Kosher salt and ground black pepper

3 medium garlic cloves, finely chopped

1½ teaspoons ground cumin

1 teaspoon Aleppo pepper or see substitute, p. 7

1 cup coarse bulgur

1 tablespoon pomegranate molasses, plus more if needed

1 pint grape tomatoes, halved

¾ cup chopped fresh mint or flat-leaf parsley

This Armenian salad, known as eetch, is heartier and more substantial than tabbouleh, the better-known bulgur salad. Instead of soaking the bulgur in water—as is done for tabbouleh—the bulgur here is cooked in a mixture of tomato paste and water, so the grains take on a red-orange hue. If you want to make the salad more tart and tangy, mix in a splash of lemon juice. For a more substantial meal, add blanched green beans and crumbled feta cheese.

Don't use fine or medium bulgur. These varieties have different liquid-absorption rates than coarse bulgur, the type called for in this recipe. They also don't have the same hearty chew.

1. In a small bowl, whisk together 1⅓ cups water and the tomato paste. Set aside. In a 10-inch skillet over medium, heat the oil until shimmering. Add the bell pepper, chopped scallions and ½ teaspoon salt. Cover and cook, stirring occasionally, until the bell pepper is tender, about 5 minutes. Stir in the garlic, cumin and Aleppo pepper, then cook until fragrant, about 1 minute.

2. Stir in the bulgur, the tomato paste mixture and 1¼ teaspoons salt. Bring to a boil over medium-high. Cover, reduce to low and cook until the bulgur has absorbed the liquid, 12 to 15 minutes. Remove from the heat and let stand, covered, for 5 minutes.

3. Transfer to a wide, shallow bowl and let cool until just warm, about 5 minutes. Drizzle the pomegranate molasses over the bulgur, then fold until combined. Fold in the tomatoes, mint and sliced scallions. Taste and season with salt, black pepper and additional pomegranate molasses.

Austrian Potato Salad

Start to finish: 30 minutes / Servings: 4

2 pounds Yukon Gold potatoes, peeled, halved and sliced ¼-inch thick

2 cups low-sodium chicken broth

Kosher salt

¼ cup finely chopped cornichons, plus 1 tablespoon brine

2 tablespoons red wine vinegar, divided

Ground black pepper

½ cup diced red onion (about ½ medium)

½ teaspoon caraway seeds

¼ cup grapeseed or other neutral oil

1 tablespoon Dijon mustard

½ cup diced celery (about 2 medium stalks)

2 hard-boiled eggs, chopped (optional)

¼ cup chopped fresh dill

Our ongoing quest to take potato salad from humdrum to humming took us to Austria, where they don't drown their potato salads in mayonnaise. In this version, the flavor starts early as the potatoes are simmered in a mixture of chicken broth and water. Onions and caraway seeds also go into the pot, softening the flavors of both. Always loath to flush flavor down the drain, we save some of the seasoned, starchy cooking liquid to help thicken a dressing made tangy with mustard, oil and vinegar. If your potatoes are quite large, quarter them instead of halving before slicing. To add crunch, we used celery; you also could add chopped hard-boiled eggs. A handful of fresh dill made for a bright finish.

Don't overcook—or undercook—the potatoes. They should be firm but not grainy, creamy in the center and just starting to fall apart at the edges. This texture is important, as some of the potatoes will break down into the salad. But if they're too soft, they will turn into mashed potatoes.

1. In a medium saucepan, combine the potatoes, broth and 2 teaspoons salt. Add enough water to just cover the potatoes. Bring to a boil over medium-high. Reduce heat to medium-low and simmer until just tender, 8 to 10 minutes. Drain, reserving ½ cup of the cooking liquid, and transfer to a large bowl. Sprinkle with the cornichon brine, 1 tablespoon of the vinegar and ½ teaspoon pepper.

2. In the empty pan, combine the reserved cooking liquid with the onion and caraway seeds and bring to a simmer over medium-high. Pour the mixture over the potatoes and stir well. Let sit, stirring occasionally, until the liquid is absorbed and thickened, about 10 minutes.

3. Meanwhile, in a liquid measuring cup, whisk together the oil, mustard, the remaining 1 tablespoon of vinegar, ¾ teaspoon salt and ½ teaspoon pepper until emulsified. To the potatoes, add the dressing, celery, eggs, if using, cornichons and dill, then fold until evenly coated. Taste and season with salt and pepper. Serve at room temperature.

Senegalese Avocado and Mango Salad with Rof

Start to finish: 30 minutes / Servings: 4

2 cups lightly packed fresh
flat-leaf parsley

4 scallions, roughly chopped

2 medium garlic cloves, peeled

1 habañero chili, stemmed and seeded

Kosher salt and ground black pepper

1 teaspoon grated lime zest,
plus ¼ cup lime juice

¼ cup roasted peanut oil

Two 14- to 16-ounce ripe mangoes,
peeled, pitted and thinly sliced

2 ripe avocados

1 cup grape tomatoes, chopped

This spicy yet refreshing salad—adapted from a recipe in Pierre Thiam's cookbook "Yolele!"—combines sweet, sour and salty flavors, accented by fresh parsley. We learned this lesson while traveling to Dakar with Thiam. The dressing is based on the Senagalese condiment known as rof, an aromatic blend of parsley, garlic, onion and chilies. It's worth seeking out roasted peanut oil for the dressing, as it adds deep, nutty notes and a rich aroma, but regular peanut oil or extra-virgin olive oil worked, too. If you have flaky sea salt, use instead of kosher salt for sprinkling on the mangoes and avocados; the crunch adds dimension to the dish.

Don't prep the avocados until you're ready to assemble the salad so that the fruit remains vibrant green for serving.

1. In a food processor, combine the parsley, scallions, garlic, habañero, 1 teaspoon salt and ½ teaspoon pepper. Process until finely chopped, about 1 minute, scraping the sides of the bowl as needed. Add the lime zest and juice and peanut oil and process until smooth, about 30 seconds.

2. In a medium bowl, combine the mango slices with 3 tablespoons of the dressing and gently toss. Marinate at room temperature for 30 minutes.

3. Lay the mango slices on a serving platter; do not wash the bowl. Halve, pit, peel and thinly slice the avocados. Arrange the avocados on top of the mangoes. Sprinkle lightly with salt and drizzle with 3 tablespoons of the remaining dressing.

4. In the same bowl used for the mangos, toss together the tomatoes and 1 tablespoon of the remaining dressing. Scatter the mixture over the mangoes and avocados. Serve with the remaining dressing on the side.

Skillet-Charred Brussels Sprouts
with Garlic, Anchovy and Chili

Start to finish: 25 minutes / Servings: 4

---

1 pound small to medium Brussels sprouts, trimmed and halved

4 tablespoons extra-virgin olive oil, divided

4 teaspoons honey, divided

Kosher salt

4 garlic cloves, minced

4 anchovy fillets, minced

Red pepper flakes

2 teaspoons lemon juice

We loved the Brussels sprouts at Gjelina, a Los Angeles restaurant. Chef Travis Lett serves them with chili-lime vinaigrette, and they are both wonderfully charred and tender. We assumed they'd been roasted in a very hot oven. In fact, Lett had used a cast-iron skillet, a quicker and more efficient way to transfer heat. We tried it and loved the way the searing-hot skillet gave the sprouts a delicious char we'd never achieved in the oven. For the sauce, we were inspired by bagna càuda, the warm garlic- and anchovy-infused dip from Northern Italy, with red pepper flakes and a splash of lemon juice. A drizzle of honey in the dressing added a note of sweetness.

Don't use a stainless steel skillet. A well-seasoned cast-iron pan was key to this recipe. Stainless steel didn't hold the heat well enough to properly char. To comfortably accommodate the recipe, the pan needed to be at least 12 inches. And stick to small or medium sprouts; large ones didn't taste as good, containing a higher concentration of the compounds that lead to bitterness. Even smaller sprouts were best when cut in half, creating more surface area and contact with the skillet and therefore more charring.

1. In a large bowl, toss the sprouts with 1 tablespoon of the oil, 2 teaspoons of the honey and ½ teaspoon of salt. Set aside.

2. In a 12- to 14-inch cast-iron skillet over high, combine the remaining 3 tablespoons of oil, the garlic, anchovies and ¼ teaspoon pepper flakes. Cook, stirring, until the garlic begins to color, 3 to 4 minutes. Scrape the mixture, including the oil, into a bowl and set aside.

3. Return the skillet to high heat. Add the sprouts (reserve the bowl) and use tongs to arrange them cut side down in a single layer. Cook, without moving, until deeply browned and blackened in spots, 3 to 7 minutes, depending on your skillet. Use the tongs to flip the sprouts cut-side up and cook until charred and just tender, another 3 to 5 minutes.

4. As they finish, return the sprouts to the bowl and toss with the garlic mixture, the remaining 2 teaspoons of honey and the lemon juice. Season with salt and additional pepper flakes.

Hot Oil–Flashed Chard with Ginger, Scallions and Chili

Start to finish: **20 minutes** / Servings: 4

¼ teaspoon kosher salt

2 large bunches Swiss chard
(1½ to 2 pounds), stems removed,
leaves sliced crosswise into
3-inch pieces

2 scallions, thinly sliced on diagonal

1 tablespoon finely grated
fresh ginger

1 serrano chili, thinly sliced

2 tablespoons grapeseed oil

1 tablespoon toasted sesame oil

1 tablespoon unseasoned
rice vinegar

1 tablespoon soy sauce

2 teaspoons toasted
sesame seeds (optional)

Most hearty greens are naturally tough and bitter, requiring extended cooking. So we tamed and tenderized Swiss chard with sizzling oil, a technique we learned from cookbook author and Chinese cuisine expert Fuchsia Dunlop. Her recipe is modeled on a classic Cantonese method in which hot oil is poured over lightly blanched greens. We scattered fresh ginger, scallions and serrano chilies over our greens and found the hot oil bloomed the flavors beautifully. Instead of julienning the ginger, as is traditional, we used a wand-style grater to finely grate it, which distributed it better, was faster and released more of the aromatics. Bonus: No fibrous pieces in the finished dish. For the oil, we found the clean flavor and light texture of grapeseed oil was ideal, but vegetable oil worked well, too. We added toasted sesame oil for a savory touch. To finish the dish, soy sauce alone is fine, but even better was a blend of soy sauce and unseasoned rice vinegar, which added a gentle acidity and light sweetness.

Don't use the chard stems, but also don't throw them away. The stems are tougher than the leaves and won't cook through in the short time it takes to wilt the leaves. Chard stems do have good flavor, however, and can be sauteed, pickled or added to soups and stews.

1. In a large skillet over medium-high, bring ¼ cup water and salt to a boil. Pile the chard into the pan and cover (the lid may not close completely). Cook until the chard is wilted, about 5 minutes, stirring halfway through. Remove the lid and cook, stirring occasionally, until most of the liquid has evaporated, 1 to 3 minutes. Transfer the chard to a serving platter and wipe out the skillet.

2. Distribute the scallions, ginger and chili evenly over the chard. Add both oils to the skillet and return to medium-high heat until very hot, 1 to 2 minutes. Pour the oils directly over the greens and aromatics (you should hear them sizzle) and toss to distribute. Drizzle the vinegar and soy sauce over the chard and toss again. Sprinkle with the sesame seeds, if using.

ADD SIZZLE
TO YOUR GREENS

Sizzling oil enhances ingredients such as scallions and grated fresh ginger because it draws out their flavors and aromas, yet leaves them tasting fresh. We used Swiss chard here, but this technique works for all manner of vegetables, from broccoli and cauliflower to tender green beans, shredded carrots and julienned sugar snap peas. More robust vegetables should be blanched first in salted water until just tender, then drained. This method also works on poached fish, shrimp, chicken or tofu.

CHINESE TABLE CLEAVERS

American home cooks typically are told the triangular Western chef's knife is the one knife to rule them all. But most of Asia favors rectangular cleaver-like knives, such as the Chinese cai dao. They typically have blades about 8 inches long and 4 inches deep and are surprisingly light. Though proficiency with them involves a learning curve, we were impressed with the way they sliced, diced, chopped, smashed, pulverized and pounded. They also were arguably the most effective bench scraper we've used.

If you're game to try one, keep a few things in mind:

• The forward weight of the blade is different from the neutral balance of a Western knife. The knife leads you rather than you leading it.

• The blade's height changes the spatial relationship between the hand you keep on the knife and the hand you keep on the cutting board. With Western knives, both hands operate on similar planes. It can be disconcerting for them to be so far apart.

• Western blades work best with a rocking motion. Asian cleaver blades are mostly flat and require more of a push or chop.

• Handle a cai dao similar to a Western chef's knife. For the best control you should pinch the blade between your thumb and forefinger while the rest of your fingers wrap around the handle.

Cracked Potatoes with Vermouth, Coriander and Fennel

Start to finish: **35 minutes (10 minutes active)** / Servings: 4

1½ pounds small Yukon Gold potatoes (1½ to 2 inches in diameter)

2 tablespoons extra-virgin olive oil, divided

1 teaspoon kosher salt

¼ teaspoon ground black pepper

1 tablespoon salted butter

2 teaspoons coriander seeds, cracked

1 teaspoon fennel seeds, cracked

1 cup dry vermouth

As much as we like them, crispy, smashed potatoes are a bother. First you boil, then flatten, then crisp in fat. And half the time our potatoes fall apart. We wanted a one-stroke solution, which we found in potatoes afelia, a Cypriot dish that calls for cracking the potatoes when raw, then braising them. Our starting point was a recipe from London chefs Sam and Sam Clark of Moro. They whack raw potatoes, causing them to split and fracture slightly, but not break apart. Next, they cook them in a covered pan with oil and coriander seeds, a traditional afelia flavoring. Red wine, added at the end, simmers into a flavorful sauce. Back at Milk Street we got cracking. Hit too hard and the potatoes break; too gently and they're merely dented. A firm, controlled hit with a meat mallet was the answer. We preferred dry vermouth to red wine. We hate opening a bottle of wine just to cook with and almost always have an open bottle of dry vermouth, which as a fortified wine lasts longer and adds a clean, herbal flavor.

Don't use a skillet with an ill-fitting lid. If the moisture evaporates too quickly, the bottom of the pan can scorch. If the pan looks dry after 10 minutes, add water 2 tablespoons at a time.

1. Using a meat mallet or the bottom of a heavy skillet, whack the potatoes one at a time to crack them until slightly flattened but still intact. In a bowl, toss the potatoes with 1 tablespoon of the oil and the salt and pepper.

2. In a 12-inch stainless steel skillet over medium-high, heat the remaining 1 tablespoon of oil and the butter. Add the potatoes in a single layer, reduce heat to medium, then cook without moving until well browned, 6 to 8 minutes. Flip and cook until well browned on the other side, about 5 minutes.

3. Add the coriander and fennel. Cook, shaking the pan constantly, until fragrant, about 1 minute. Add the vermouth. Cover and reduce heat to medium-low. Cook until the potatoes are just tender and the liquid has nearly evaporated, 12 to 14 minutes, flipping the potatoes halfway through. Transfer to a serving bowl, scraping the sauce and seeds on top.

Sweet Potato Gratin with Vanilla Bean and Bay Leaves

Start to finish: **3 hours (50 minutes active), plus cooling** / Servings: **8**

5 pounds sweet potatoes

1 cup heavy cream

4 bay leaves

1 vanilla bean

⅓ cup plus 1 tablespoon packed dark brown sugar, divided

1¼ teaspoons kosher salt

¾ teaspoon ground black pepper

⅓ cup white sugar

Pinch cayenne pepper

Sweet potato casserole is a Thanksgiving staple, but our version is delicious all year. We start by ditching the marshmallows and upping the flavor with a dash of spice. For ease, we roasted the sweet potatoes, a hands-off process that can be done a day ahead. Roasting rather than boiling produces cleaner, deeper flavors and a better, less watery texture. In lieu of marshmallows we infuse cream with vanilla bean and bay leaves and add a dusting of black pepper. A crunchy topping of dark brown and white sugar with a touch of cayenne keeps the dish appropriate for the adults' table.

Don't get distracted while the gratin is broiling; all broilers are different, and the difference between browned and burnt can be a matter of seconds.

1. Heat the oven to 400°F with one rack in the middle and another 6 inches from the broiler. Pierce the sweet potatoes with a fork and arrange on a rimmed baking sheet. Bake on the middle rack, turning once, until tender, 1 to 1½ hours. Let cool. Increase oven to 425°F.

2. Meanwhile, in a medium saucepan, combine the cream and bay leaves. With a paring knife, split the vanilla bean lengthwise, then scrape out the seeds. Add the seeds and pod to the cream and bring to a simmer over medium-high. Set aside, covered, for 30 minutes. Strain out and discard the solids.

3. Once the potatoes have cooled, scrape the flesh from the skins; discard the skins. In a food processor, combine half the flesh and half the infused cream. Add 1 tablespoon of the brown sugar, the salt and pepper. Process until smooth, about 1 minute, scraping the

bowl halfway through; transfer to a large bowl. Repeat with the remaining potatoes and cream, then add to the first batch. Mix well, then transfer to a 13-by-9-inch broiler safe baking dish. Smooth the top.

4. In a bowl, stir together the remaining ⅓ cup of brown sugar, the white sugar and the cayenne. Transfer to a medium mesh strainer, then evenly sift the mixture over the surface of the potatoes (or do by hand). Brush any sugar off the rim of the baking dish.

5. Bake on the middle rack until bubbling at the edges, about 20 minutes. Remove from the oven, then heat the broiler. When ready, place the dish on the upper rack and broil until deeply browned and crisp, 2 to 7 minutes. Let sit for 20 minutes before serving.

Celery Root Puree

Start to finish: **45 minutes** / Servings: **8**

2 pounds celery root, peeled and cut into 1-inch pieces

1 pound Yukon Gold potatoes, peeled and cut into 1-inch pieces

2 cups half-and-half

2 cups whole milk

4 garlic cloves, smashed and peeled

4 sprigs fresh thyme

Kosher salt

8 tablespoons (1 stick) salted butter

Ground black pepper

Chopped fresh chives

THE MATTER OF THE ROOT

Between its lumpy shape, thick skin and gnarly tangle of roots, celery root can be a real challenge, but not an insurmountable one. To start, use a strong knife to chop off the bottom (root end) of the bulb. Use a Y-style peeler to peel and discard the skin (you may need to use a paring knife for thicker skins). Cut out any discolored veins that may be left. Once peeled, cut the root into chunks to be used as is—as we do in our celery puree—or thinly slice using a mandolin or food processor to use fresh in a salad, such as a classic French remoulade.

We give mashed potatoes a sophisticated spin with an unlikely candidate: celery root. Also known as celeriac, this vegetable gets little attention in American kitchens—perhaps because of its less than beautiful appearance. When cooked and processed, however, the knobby, gnarled root transforms into a subtler, version of mashed potatoes with a light, fresh celery flavor. To balance that lightness, we paired celery root with Yukon Golds, producing a medium-bodied puree. We cooked the vegetables in a mixture of milk and half-and-half, a combination that won't dilute or mask celery root's flavor. A stick of butter gave the puree a silky texture. We liked the flavors of thyme and garlic, but small amounts of sage, rosemary and marjoram worked, too. The cooled puree can be refrigerated for two days; rewarm in a saucepan over low heat and check the seasoning before serving.

Don't add too much cooking liquid right away as the moisture content of starchy vegetables can vary. If your puree is loose, start with just a splash and go from there.

1. In a large saucepan over high, combine the celery root, potatoes, half-and-half, milk, garlic, thyme and 1½ teaspoons salt. Bring to a boil, then cover, leaving the lid slightly ajar, and reduce heat to low. Simmer, stirring occasionally, until the vegetables are tender, about 25 minutes. The mixture will froth and foam and may appear curdled; watch carefully to prevent boiling over.

2. Drain the vegetables, reserving the liquid. Remove and discard the thyme sprigs, then transfer the solids to a food processor. Process until smooth, about 1 minute. Return to the pan along with the butter. Set over low heat and cook, stirring occasionally, until the butter is melted. Starting with ½ cup, gradually stir in the reserved cooking liquid until the puree reaches the desired consistency. The puree should be not quite pourable. Taste and season with salt and pepper. Sprinkle with chives.

Sweet-and-Spicy Ginger Green Beans

Start to finish: **10 minutes** / Servings: **4**

2 tablespoons packed
light brown sugar

1 tablespoon fish sauce

1 tablespoon soy sauce

3 tablespoons grapeseed
or other neutral oil, divided

1 pound green beans, stemmed
and halved crosswise on diagonal

1 tablespoon finely grated
fresh ginger

½ teaspoon red pepper flakes

2 tablespoons unseasoned
rice vinegar

Ground white pepper

The challenge of stir-frying green beans is that, more often than not, the frills slide off and you're left biting into a bland bean. The key is cooking them in a sauce that actually sticks. Chef Charles Phan, owner of The Slanted Door, a popular Vietnamese restaurant in San Francisco, caramelizes sugar, then stir-fries string beans in the blistering heat of a wok. A final toss with sake and fish sauce coats the charred beans with a dark, bittersweet sauce. We adjusted the recipe to work without a wok. Phan's recipe calls for blanching the beans first. We simplified by adding the beans to a very hot pan with a small amount of oil, then making a sauce around them as they cooked. We found a Dutch oven worked best to control splattering—drying the beans thoroughly also helped (though a large skillet works in a pinch). Cutting the beans on a bias gave us more surface area for better browning. To re-create Phan's flavorful sauce—itself a take on nuoc mau, or Vietnamese caramel sauce—we used brown sugar instead of taking the time to caramelize white sugar. It gave us comparable depth and flavor.

Don't use an ill-fitting lid. A proper seal is key to this recipe, whether you cook the beans in a Dutch oven or a skillet. Have the lid ready as soon as you add the water.

1. In a small bowl, stir together the sugar, fish and soy sauces. Set aside.

2. In a large Dutch oven or 12-inch skillet over medium-high, heat 2 tablespoons of the oil until beginning to smoke. Add the beans and cook, without stirring, until beginning to color, about 3 minutes. Add ¼ cup water and immediately cover the pan. Cook until the beans are bright green and barely tender, about 2 minutes.

3. Clear a space in the center of the pan, then add the remaining 1 tablespoon of oil to the clearing. Stir in the ginger and pepper flakes, then cook until fragrant, about 30 seconds. Stir the sugar-fish sauce mixture then pour it into the skillet and cook, stirring occasionally, until the liquid has thickened and coats the beans, about 1 minute. Off heat, stir in the vinegar. Taste and season with pepper.

Mashed Potatoes with Caraway-Mustard Butter

Start to finish: 40 minutes (10 minutes active) / Servings: 8

4 pounds Yukon Gold potatoes, peeled and quartered

Kosher salt

5 bay leaves

4 medium garlic cloves, smashed and peeled

10 tablespoons (1¼ sticks) salted butter, divided

1¾ cups half-and-half, warmed

½ cup drained prepared white horseradish, liquid reserved

1 tablespoon caraway seeds, lightly crushed

1 tablespoon yellow mustard seeds

2 tablespoons finely chopped chives

These mashed potatoes are classically creamy, but get a kick of sweet heat from horseradish. Infusing browned butter with caraway and mustard seeds and drizzling the mixture onto the mashed potatoes is a technique we picked up from Indian cooking. The spices add a complexity that balances the richness of the dish. We preferred buttery Yukon Gold potatoes; use potatoes of approximately the same size to ensure even cooking. Any brand of refrigerated prepared horseradish worked well.

Don't rush browning the butter. It needs to cook slowly over medium heat to properly brown (you'll see brown spots on the bottom of the saucepan).

1. In a large pot, combine the potatoes, 1 tablespoon salt, the bay leaves and garlic. Add enough water to cover by 2 inches and bring to a boil over high. Reduce to medium, then cook until a skewer inserted into the potatoes meets no resistance, 20 to 25 minutes. Drain the potatoes in a colander set in the sink. Discard the bay leaves, then return the potatoes to the pot.

2. In a small saucepan over medium-low, melt 6 tablespoons of the butter. Add the melted butter to the potatoes. Using a potato masher, mash until smooth. Stir in the half-and-half, horseradish and 3 tablespoons of the reserved horseradish liquid. Taste and season with salt. Cover and set over low heat to keep warm.

3. Return the saucepan to medium and add the remaining 4 tablespoons butter and the caraway and mustard seeds. Cook, gently swirling the pan, until the butter is browned and the seeds are fragrant and toasted, 2 to 3 minutes. Pour the mixture into fine mesh strainer set over a small liquid measuring cup.

4. Transfer the potatoes to a serving bowl, then drizzle with the flavored butter and sprinkle with chives.

Cauliflower with Tahini and Egyptian Nut-and-Seed Seasoning (*Dukkah*)

Start to finish: **35 minutes** / Servings: **4**

½ cup tahini

1 teaspoon grated lemon zest, plus 2 tablespoons lemon juice, divided

2 tablespoons extra-virgin olive oil, plus more to serve

2 garlic cloves, grated

1½ teaspoons kosher salt

1 teaspoon sweet paprika

¼ to ½ teaspoon cayenne pepper

1 large head cauliflower (about 2½ pounds), cut into 1½- to 2-inch florets

⅓ cup roasted, salted cashews, chopped

⅓ cup chopped fresh cilantro

Cauliflower's been getting the celebrity treatment lately, but we liked it before it was cool for its mild, nutty flavor. In this take, we roasted florets with a tahini sauce brightened with lemon juice and cayenne. We used cilantro in our sauce, but flat-leaf parsley worked as a substitute. When buying cauliflower, look for a head with densely packed florets. Medium florets, about 1½ to 2 inches, were best in this dish; smaller pieces became mushy. And a hot oven and heated baking sheet were key to browning the cauliflower before it overcooked. For a crunchy, nutty alternative, substitute ⅓ cup dukkah (see sidebar) for the cashews.

Don't forget to line the baking sheet with foil before heating. The tahini mixture makes a mess of an unlined pan.

1. Heat the oven to 500°F with a rack in the lowest position. Line a rimmed baking sheet with foil and set on the rack to heat. In a large bowl, whisk together the tahini, lemon zest, 1 tablespoon of the lemon juice, the oil, garlic, salt, paprika and cayenne. Add the cauliflower and toss, massaging the dressing into the florets.

2. Working quickly, remove the baking sheet from the oven and carefully spread the cauliflower on it in an even layer, scraping any remaining tahini onto the florets.

Reserve the bowl. Roast until well browned in spots and just tender, 15 to 18 minutes, stirring and turning the florets and rotating the pan halfway through.

3. Transfer the roasted florets to the reserved bowl. Add the remaining 1 tablespoon of lemon juice and toss. Add half of the nuts and the cilantro and toss. Sprinkle with the remaining cashews and serve drizzled with more oil, if desired.

EGYPTIAN NUT-AND-SEED SEASONING (DUKKAH)

The Egyptian seasoning mixture known as dukkah—a rich blend of seeds, nuts and spices—adds welcome texture and complexity to dips and salads, and even can be used as a rub for meat or fish. It began as peasant fare, used to give flavor to coarse bread. In the U.S., dukkah has found popularity with restaurant chefs. It can be bought ready-made from spice shops (and Trader Joe's), but the best way to enjoy it is to make your own. Store in an airtight container at room temperature for up to a week. Freeze for longer use.

Start to finish: **15 minutes**
Makes **about 1 cup**

½ cup raw cashews

2 tablespoons sesame seeds

2 tablespoons coriander seeds

2 tablespoons cumin seeds

1 tablespoon caraway seeds

1 teaspoon dried oregano

½ teaspoon kosher salt

½ teaspoon ground black pepper

In a large skillet over medium, toast the cashews, stirring, until beginning to brown, 3 to 4 minutes. Add the sesame seeds and toast, stirring, until golden, 1 to 2 minutes. Add the coriander, cumin and caraway, and toast, stirring, until fragrant, about 1 minute. Transfer to a food processor and let cool for 5 minutes. Add the oregano, salt and pepper. Pulse until coarsely ground, 12 to 15 pulses.

Harissa Roasted Potatoes

Start to finish: 1 hour (10 minutes active) / Servings: 4

2 pounds Yukon Gold potatoes, peeled and cut into 1½-inch pieces

4 ounces shallots (about 4 small), peeled and quartered

2 tablespoons extra-virgin olive oil

1 teaspoon kosher salt

½ teaspoon ground black pepper

6 tablespoons harissa, divided (recipe p. 362)

⅓ cup chopped flat-leaf fresh parsley

1 tablespoon lemon juice, plus lemon wedges to serve

Harissa (pronounced ha-REE-sah) may well be one of the original hot sauces. It's generally believed to have originated in Tunisia, where it's often served with couscous and brik, a tuna-and-egg turnover. This recipe uses our piquant, homemade harissa sauce (p. 362) to give potatoes a sweet-spicy kick, but harissa also can be found online and in the grocer's international aisle. Tossing the raw potatoes with harissa before roasting muted the chili paste's flavor, so we crisped "naked" potatoes on the bottom rack first, then tossed them with a portion of the harissa and returned them to the oven. That gave the potatoes the right texture and a spicy crust. A final hit of the remaining harissa, along with parsley and lemon juice, kept the flavors bright.

Don't forget to taste your harissa for heat and pungency before tossing the potatoes. A harissa with gentle heat and smooth texture, like Milk Street's recipe, worked best here. If your variety is particularly spicy, you may want to reduce the total amount to ¼ cup, reserving 1 tablespoon to finish the dish.

1. Heat the oven to 400°F with racks in the middle and lowest positions and a rimmed baking sheet on the bottom rack. In a large bowl, toss the potatoes and shallots with the oil, salt and pepper.

2. Working quickly, remove the baking sheet from the oven, add the potato-shallot mixture and spread in an even layer; reserve the bowl. Roast on the bottom rack until the potatoes are well browned on the bottoms, about 20 minutes, rotating the sheet halfway through.

3. Use a thin metal spatula to transfer the potatoes to the reserved bowl, scraping up any browned bits. Add 4 tablespoons of the harissa and toss until evenly coated. Return the potatoes to the sheet, spreading in an even layer and reserving the bowl. Roast on the middle rack until tender, 18 to 22 minutes, rotating the sheet halfway through.

4. Return the potatoes to the reserved bowl, scraping up any browned bits from the pan. Add the parsley, the remaining 2 tablespoons of harissa and the lemon juice. Toss to coat. Serve with lemon wedges.

Grains

5

Quinoa Pilaf with Dates, Almonds and Carrot Juice

Start to finish: 40 minutes (15 minutes active) / Servings: 4

2 tablespoons salted butter

1 medium carrot, peeled and diced (about ½ cup)

1 small yellow onion, diced (about ½ cup)

Kosher salt

1 cup white quinoa

1 tablespoon finely grated fresh ginger

1 teaspoon ground cumin

½ cup carrot juice

4 medjool dates, pitted and diced

⅓ cup chopped almonds or cashews, toasted

2 scallions, trimmed and chopped

3 tablespoons chopped fresh dill, plus more to garnish

1 teaspoon grated lemon zest, plus 1 tablespoon lemon juice

Ground black pepper

Extra-virgin olive oil, for drizzling (optional)

We like the nutty, earthy flavor and gentle crunch of quinoa, but too often salads made with this seed—it's technically not a grain—end up mushy and flavorless. For a better way, we looked to Deborah Madison, author of "Vegetarian Cooking for Everyone." She cooks her quinoa in carrot juice, a winning combination that perked up its natural sweetness and tempered its tendency to muddiness. We also liked a quinoa by Erik Ramirez of Brooklyn's Llama Inn. He makes a famously madcap quinoa pilaf studded with bananas, bacon, cashews and avocado, which showed us that texture and contrast can make the often insipid seed exciting. We liked a simple combo of chewy-sweet dates and crunchy almonds. We took a three-step approach to keeping our pilaf light and fluffy: first toasting the quinoa, then cooking it with less liquid than typically called for, and finally letting the cooked quinoa rest before fluffing. For texture, we added dates and almonds or cashews; both worked. Finishing with scallions, lemon and fresh dill brightened the final dish. Eat this as is or pair it with sautéed shrimp, broiled salmon or fried tofu.

Don't worry about rinsing the quinoa. Most varieties sold in the U.S. are pre-rinsed. Just check the packaging.

1. In a medium saucepan over medium, melt the butter. Add the carrot, onion and ¼ teaspoon salt. Cook, stirring, until softened, 3 to 5 minutes. Add the quinoa and cook, stirring, until fragrant and beginning to pop, about 5 minutes. Stir in the ginger and cumin. Cook, stirring, for 1 minute. Add the carrot juice, ¾ cup water and ½ teaspoon salt. Bring to a boil. Cover, reduce to medium-low and cook until the liquid is absorbed, 11 to 13 minutes.

2. Remove the pan from the heat and uncover. Sprinkle in the dates, cover the pan with a kitchen towel and replace the lid. Let sit for 10 minutes. Fluff the quinoa with a fork, then add the almonds or cashews, scallions, dill, lemon zest and juice. Stir gently to combine, season with salt and pepper, then garnish with dill and a drizzle of olive oil, if desired.

LIKE CARROT JUICE FOR WATER

Substituting another liquid for water when cooking lets you nudge the flavor factor up a notch with little effort. In our quinoa pilaf, for example, we cook the seeds in diluted carrot juice, which mitigates their subtle bitterness. And for our Chinese white-cooked chicken (p. 220), we recommend cooking an accompanying pot of rice in the warm broth generated by the cooked bird, infusing the meal with every bit of meaty flavor. This works for sweets, too. Our caramel oranges (p. 320) get added depth by swapping fresh orange juice for the water typically used to dissolve the sugar for the caramel sauce. Try this different ways. Use broth or diluted vegetable juices to cook grains, or puree soft fresh herbs and a garlic clove or two in water, then use that to cook rice or bulgur. Be mindful that acidic ingredients can change the rate at which starches cook. You can add tomato flavor to rice as we do in our Indian tomato rice (p. 137), but don't try to cook rice in tomato juice; the rice will turn out mushy and unevenly cooked.

Thai Fried Rice

Start to finish: **20 minutes** / Servings: **4**

1 tablespoon fish sauce

1 teaspoon soy sauce

1 teaspoon white sugar

4 cups cooked and chilled jasmine rice

1 tablespoon peanut or vegetable oil

2 eggs, lightly beaten

4 ounces thinly sliced pancetta, chopped

4 scallions, white and green parts thinly sliced, reserved separately

1 large shallot, minced

1 garlic clove, minced

¼ cup chopped fresh cilantro

Sliced cucumber and lime wedges, to serve

Cooked in under five minutes in the open-air kitchen of his home in Thailand, chef Andy Ricker's fried rice was speedy, simple—and delicious. Pork belly, shallot and garlic added bold flavors. Soy and fish sauces added savory depth. Fresh herbs kept everything bright and light. We returned to Milk Street and got to work deconstructing Thai cooking. Ricker prefers to use a wok because it allows him to move food away from the hot oil at the center to the cooler sides of the pan. In a nod to the Western kitchen, we began with a large nonstick skillet, though you can use a wok if you have one (and a burner powerful enough to heat it). Pork belly can be hard to find in the U.S. Looking for a substitute we found ground pork too greasy and bacon too smoky. Pancetta—if culturally odd—was just right, which makes sense since it's cured pork belly. In a skillet, we had to reverse-engineer the process and move foods in and out, starting with the eggs, then the pancetta. We liked the aromatic flavor of jasmine rice, but long-grain white or basmati work, too. If you have no leftover rice, follow our recipe (see sidebar). Thai restaurants offer condiments for fried rice, including sliced green chilies in white vinegar. We came up with our own (p. 389). Use it with the fried rice or any dish that needs a hit of gentle heat and acid.

Don't use hot or warm rice. The fried rice will be clumpy and gummy (see sidebar).

1. In a bowl, stir together the fish sauce, soy sauce, 1 teaspoon water and sugar. Set aside. Use your hands to break up the rice so no clumps remain. Set aside.

2. In a 12-inch nonstick skillet over medium-high, heat the oil until barely smoking. Pour in the eggs and cook, stirring, until just set. Transfer the eggs to a plate. Add the pancetta to the skillet and cook over medium until crisp. Using a slotted spoon, transfer to the plate with the eggs.

3. Pour off all but 1 tablespoon of the fat from the skillet and return to medium-high. Add the scallion whites, shallot and garlic and cook until softened, about 1 minute. Add the rice and cook, stirring occasionally, until heated through, about 2 minutes.

4. Stir the fish sauce mixture, then pour over the rice. Cook, stirring, until well mixed. Stir in the egg and pancetta, breaking up the eggs. Transfer to a large platter and sprinkle with cilantro and scallion greens. Serve with cucumber, lime wedges and fish sauce–pickled chilies (p. 389), if desired.

RICE AT THE READY

While our Thai fried rice takes just minutes to prepare, it does require cooked-and-cooled plain rice. Warm, freshly cooked rice won't work; it sticks to the pan and turns gummy. For rice to fry, its starches must first cool and recrystallize. Fresh rice needed two hours minimum to chill adequately, but it can be prepared up to three days in advance and kept refrigerated. For real make-ahead convenience, cooked rice also can be frozen. Make a batch or two, then freeze in zip-close plastic bags.

Rice for Thai Fried Rice

Start to finish: 20 minutes,
plus cooling
Makes 4 cups

2 cups water

1½ cups jasmine rice, rinsed

½ teaspoon kosher salt

Line a rimmed baking sheet with kitchen parchment and lightly coat it with vegetable oil. In a large saucepan, combine the water, rice and salt. Bring to a simmer, then reduce to low, cover and cook until tender and fluffy, 15 to 18 minutes. Fluff with a fork, then spread on the prepared baking sheet. Let cool, then cover and refrigerate until cold.

Coconut Rice

Start to finish: **35 minutes (10 minutes active)** / Servings: 4

___

2 tablespoons coconut oil, preferably unrefined

½ cup unsweetened shredded coconut

1½ cups jasmine rice, rinsed

14-ounce can coconut milk, shaken

1 teaspoon kosher salt

Plain rice needs to be paired with a flavorful counterpoint, otherwise it's just a bowl of bland. Fiery curries, for example, are a great partner. But what if you're not into (or in the mood for) heat? We found our flavor in coconut rice, a dish popular in India and Southeast Asia, where it appears in many forms. It's quick and easy to assemble and has layers of flavor. We start by toasting unsweetened coconut in coconut oil, which gave us a pleasant texture as well as flavor. The rice went in next and we added unsweetened coconut milk at two stages: as the rice cooked and at the very end. We chose jasmine rice for its aromatic flavor. Gentle heat ensured the liquid wouldn't boil over and the rice wouldn't burn on the bottom. Our finished rice made the perfect accompaniment to grilled or roasted meats and fish. We like to cook extra and use leftovers in fried rice, salads or to pair with fried eggs for breakfast. It's even good as a sweet snack with a sprinkle of brown sugar or drizzle of honey.

Don't use a small saucepan. If the cooking liquid bubbles over, the sugar will cause it to smoke and burn. A medium or large heavy-bottomed saucepan was best.

1. In a medium saucepan over medium, combine the oil and shredded coconut. Cook, stirring, until lightly toasted, 1 to 2 minutes. Add the rice and cook, stirring, until some of the grains are translucent and a few begin to pop, about 2 minutes. Stir in ¾ cup water, all but 2 tablespoons of the coconut milk and the salt.

2. Bring to a simmer, stirring and scraping the bottom of the pan frequently. Reduce heat to low, cover and cook until the liquid is absorbed, 15 to 18 minutes. Remove from the heat and let sit, covered, for 5 minutes. Drizzle in the reserved coconut milk, then fluff and stir.

Japanese-Style Rice with Flaked Salmon and Shiitake Mushrooms (*Sake to Kinoko Takikomi Gohan*)

Start to finish: **50 minutes (20 minutes active)** / Servings: 4

¼ cup soy sauce

3 tablespoons sake

1 tablespoon mirin

One 6-ounce skinless salmon fillet

2 cups Japanese-style short-grain white rice, rinsed well and drained

4 ounces fresh shiitake mushrooms, stemmed and thinly sliced

3 scallions, thinly sliced on diagonal, whites and greens reserved separately

Kosher salt

Lemon wedges, to serve

This recipe is our version of a dish we learned from Elizabeth Andoh. The salmon here is thinly sliced and marinated in a mixture of soy sauce, sake and mirin, and it serves more as a flavoring for the rice than as a feature protein. After the fish marinates, the soy mixture is repurposed as a seasoning for the rice as it steams. Layering the salmon slices onto the rice after cooking and giving the rice a final quick burst of medium-high heat ensures the fish doesn't dry out. If you like, serve the rice with lemon wedges and additional soy sauce.

Don't use a saucepan with a loose-fitting lid. For the rice to cook properly, the lid must fit securely. If the lid has a vent hole, plug it with a bit of foil to prevent steam from escaping.

1. In a small bowl, stir together the soy sauce, sake and mirin. Holding your knife at a 45-degree angle to the cutting board, cut the salmon crosswise into ⅛-inch-thick slices. Add to the soy sauce mixture and gently toss. Cover and refrigerate for at least 20 minutes or up to 1 hour.

2. In a medium saucepan, combine the rice, mushrooms, scallion whites, 1 teaspoon salt and 1¾ cups water. Drain the salmon marinade into the rice and stir to combine; return the salmon to the refrigerator. Cover the pan and bring to a boil over high; this should take about 5 minutes. Reduce to low and cook for another 5 minutes.

3. Without lifting the lid, remove the pot from the heat and let stand for at least 10 minutes or up to 30 minutes. Uncover and arrange the salmon slices in an even layer on the surface of the rice. Cover and cook over medium-high until the salmon begins to turn opaque at the edges, about 1 minute. Remove from heat and let stand, covered, until the salmon is fully opaque, another 1 to 2 minutes.

4. Run a silicone spatula around the edge of the pan to loosen the rice. Gently lift and fluff the grains, flaking the fish and mixing it into the rice. Make sure to scrape along the bottom of the pan. Spoon into bowls, sprinkle with the scallion greens and serve with lemon wedges.

Coconut-Ginger Rice

Start to finish: 30 minutes / Servings: 4

---

1 tablespoon coconut oil
(preferably unrefined)

2 medium shallots, halved
and thinly sliced

1-inch piece fresh ginger, peeled,
sliced into thirds and lightly bruised

1 stalk lemon grass, trimmed to the
lower 6 inches, dry outer leaves
discarded, lightly bruised

1½ cups jasmine rice, rinsed
and drained

½ cup coconut milk

Kosher salt

Jasmine rice steamed with shallots, ginger, lemon grass and coconut yields a richly aromatic side dish that's perfect with Southeast Asian mains, such as seafood curries. Rice cooked with all coconut milk was too rich and heavy. A combination of water and coconut milk made for fluffy grains that were light yet robustly flavored. Using unrefined coconut oil reinforced the coconut flavor.

Don't use the rice without first rinsing and draining. Rinsing removes excess starch that would otherwise make the cooked grains heavy and gluey.

1. In a large saucepan over medium-high, heat the oil until barely smoking. Add the shallots and cook, stirring frequently, until lightly browned, 3 to 5 minutes. Stir in the ginger and lemon grass and cook until fragrant, about 30 seconds.

2. Stir in the rice, 1½ cups water, the coconut milk and 1 teaspoon salt, then bring to a simmer. Cover, reduce to low and cook until the rice absorbs the liquid, 15 to 20 minutes.

3. Remove and discard the ginger and lemon grass, then fluff the rice with a fork. Taste and season with salt.

Herb-and-Pistachio Couscous

Start to finish: **30 minutes** / Servings: 6

1 cup couscous

3 tablespoons dried currants

½ teaspoon ground cumin

Kosher salt and ground black pepper

¾ cup boiling water

6 tablespoons extra-virgin olive oil, divided, plus more for serving

2 cups lightly packed fresh cilantro leaves and tender stems

2 cups lightly packed fresh flat-leaf parsley leaves

2 tablespoons finely chopped pickled jalapeños, plus 2 teaspoons brine

2 ounces baby arugula, coarsely chopped (about 2 cups)

½ cup shelled pistachios, toasted and chopped

2 scallions, trimmed and thinly sliced

Couscous may be fast and convenient to prepare, but it's also pretty dull. And the traditional method of infusing it with flavor—steaming it in a special pot over a flavorful liquid—just isn't happening. We found a better way by undercooking—technically underhydrating—the couscous by preparing it with less water than typically called for. We then combine the couscous with a flavorful paste made from oil and pureed fresh herbs. The "thirsty" couscous absorbs tons of flavor as it finishes hydrating. Inspired by a recipe from Yotam Ottolenghi, we piled on the herbs—2 cups each of cilantro and flat-leaf parsley plus another 2 cups of arugula. We also added currants as we doused the couscous with boiling water, giving them time to plump. Jalapeños brought a spicy kick; we used pickled peppers, which have more consistent heat and contributed welcome piquancy. Toasted pistachios and thinly sliced scallions added a finishing crunch. The couscous pairs well with most any meat, though it is particularly good with salmon.

Don't use Israeli (also called pearl) couscous, which won't hydrate sufficiently in this recipe.

1. In a large bowl, combine the couscous, currants, cumin and ¼ teaspoon each salt and black pepper. Stir in the boiling water and 1 tablespoon of the oil, then cover and let sit for 10 minutes.

2. Meanwhile, in a food processor, combine the cilantro, parsley, the remaining 5 tablespoons of oil, the jalapeño brine and ¼ teaspoon salt. Process until a smooth paste forms, about 1 minute, scraping down the bowl 2 or 3 times.

3. Fluff the couscous with a fork, breaking up any large clumps, then stir in the herb paste until thoroughly combined. Fold in the jalapeños, arugula, pistachios and scallions, then let sit for 10 minutes. Season with salt and pepper. Serve at room temperature, drizzled with oil.

Indian Tomato Rice

Start to finish: 35 minutes (15 minutes active) / Servings: 4

1 cup white basmati rice, rinsed and drained

2 tablespoons tomato paste

2 tablespoons grapeseed or other neutral oil

1 teaspoon cumin seeds

1 teaspoon coriander seeds

1 teaspoon brown or black mustard seeds

2 bird's eye chilies, stemmed and halved lengthwise (optional)

1 garlic clove, finely grated

1 teaspoon finely grated fresh ginger

1½ teaspoons kosher salt

½ pound cherry or grape tomatoes, quartered

¼ cup chopped fresh cilantro leaves

Robust tomato flavor is key to this popular southern Indian dish, typically prepared when there is an abundance of ripe, red tomatoes and leftover basmati rice. It can be eaten as a light meal with a dollop of yogurt or pairs well with seafood, poultry or even a simple fried egg. We needed a year-round recipe, so we concentrated on finding the best way to impart deep tomato flavor. A combination of cherry or grape tomatoes and tomato paste was best. We also focused on making sure the rice was cooked properly, fluffy and tender with each grain separate. We were inspired by Madhur Jaffrey's tomato rice recipe in "Vegetarian India," though we upped the intensity of both the spices and tomato flavor. We preferred brown or black mustard seeds for their pungency; if you substitute yellow mustard seeds, increase the volume to 1½ teaspoons. Serrano chilies can be used in place of bird's eye chilies, also called Thai bird or Thai chilies. Or you can leave them out entirely. If your pan does not have a tight-fitting lid, cover it with foil before putting the lid in place.

Don't skip soaking the rice. This traditional approach to cooking the rice gives it time to expand gently and cook up in tender, separate grains.

1. In a bowl, combine the rinsed rice with enough cold water to cover by 1 inch. Let soak for 15 minutes. Drain the rice very well. In a 2-cup liquid measuring cup, combine 1¼ cups water and the tomato paste and whisk until dissolved. Set aside.

2. In a large saucepan over medium, combine the oil, cumin, coriander, mustard seeds, chilies, garlic and ginger. Cook until the seeds begin to pop and the mixture is fragrant, about 1 minute.

3. Stir in the rice and salt and cook, stirring, until coated with oil, about 30 seconds. Stir in the water-tomato paste mixture and bring to a simmer. Cover, reduce heat to low and cook until the water has been absorbed, about 15 minutes. Remove from the heat, add the tomatoes and let sit, covered, for 5 minutes. Stir in the cilantro, fluffing the rice with a fork.

Suppers

6

Punjabi Chickpeas with Potato (*Chole*)

Start to finish: 45 minutes
Servings: 4

1 large red onion

4 tablespoons grapeseed or other neutral oil, divided

1½ teaspoons ground coriander

1 teaspoon ground cardamom

1 teaspoon sweet paprika

½ teaspoon cinnamon

¼ teaspoon ground cloves

¼ teaspoon nutmeg

⅛ teaspoon cayenne pepper

Kosher salt and ground black pepper

1 teaspoon cumin seeds

¾ pound russet potatoes (about 2 medium potatoes), peeled and cut into ½-inch cubes

1 tablespoon finely grated fresh ginger

3 garlic cloves, finely grated

1 tablespoon tomato paste

Two 15½-ounce cans chickpeas, drained

1 tablespoon lime juice, plus lime wedges, to serve

¼ cup coarsely chopped cilantro leaves, plus more to garnish

Chopped fresh tomato, thinly sliced bird's eye or serrano chilies and whole-milk Greek-style yogurt, to serve (optional)

Seasoning blends known as masalas are the backbone of much of Indian cooking. But they often involve intimidatingly long lists of spices, each requiring toasting and grinding. Buying prepared blends is easier, but they can taste faded and stale. For our chole (pronounced CHO-lay)—a chickpea curry popular in India and Pakistan—we mix our own garam masala, a warm seasoning blend that features cayenne pepper and cinnamon. To make the sauce, we started with onion cooked until it practically melted. Grating the onion before browning helped it cook faster and gave it a better texture. Amchoor powder made from dried green mangoes gives traditional chole its characteristic tang, but we found lime juice was a good—and more convenient—substitute. When preparing this dish, make sure your potato pieces are no larger than ½ inch thick so they cook in time. Chole typically is eaten with flatbread, such as roti or naan.

Don't use a nonstick skillet for this recipe; the fond (browned bits on the bottom of the pan) won't form, which will alter the chole's flavor. And don't be deterred by the lengthy list of spices here. Most are pantry staples and are key to producing the dish's complex flavor.

1. Using the large holes of a box grater, grate the onion, then transfer to a mesh strainer and drain. In a small bowl, stir together 1 tablespoon of the oil with the coriander, cardamom, paprika, cinnamon, cloves, nutmeg, cayenne, 1¼ teaspoons salt and ½ teaspoon pepper.

2. In a 12-inch skillet over medium-high, heat the remaining 3 tablespoons of oil. Add the cumin seeds and cook, shaking the pan, until the seeds are fragrant and darken, 30 to 60 seconds. Add the drained onion and cook, stirring frequently, until the moisture has evaporated, 1 to 3 minutes. Add the potatoes, reduce heat to medium and cook, stirring frequently, until the onions begin to brown and a fond forms on the bottom of the pan, 6 to 8 minutes. Add the ginger, garlic and tomato paste, then cook for 1 minute, stirring constantly.

3. Clear the center of the pan, then add the spice paste to the clearing and cook, mashing and stirring until fragrant, about 15 seconds. Stir into the vegetables. Add 1½ cups water and bring to a boil, scraping up all the browned bits. Add the chickpeas and return to a boil, then cover, reduce heat to low and cook until the potatoes are tender and the oil separates from the sauce at the edges of the pan, 13 to 15 minutes.

4. Off the heat, stir in the lime juice and cilantro. Taste and season with salt and pepper. Serve with lime wedges, chopped tomato, chilies and yogurt, if desired.

Spanish Spice-Crusted Pork Tenderloin Bites (*Pinchos Morunos*)

Start to finish: **50 minutes (25 minutes active)** / Servings: 4

1½ teaspoons ground coriander

1½ teaspoons ground cumin

1½ teaspoons smoked paprika

¾ teaspoon each kosher salt and coarsely ground black pepper

1-pound pork tenderloin, trimmed of silver skin and cut into 1- to 1½-inch pieces

1 tablespoon lemon juice, plus lemon wedges for serving

1 tablespoon honey

1 medium garlic clove, finely grated

2 tablespoons extra-virgin olive oil, divided

1 tablespoon chopped fresh oregano

Loosely translated as "Moorish bites impaled on thorns or small pointed sticks," pinchos morunos is a Basque dish of seared pork tenderloin rubbed with a blend of spices, garlic, herbs and olive oil. The recipe dates back generations, boasting influences from Spain and North Africa. Classic versions skewer the meat, which is seasoned with ras el hanout, a Moroccan spice blend, among other flavorings. We streamlined, nixing the skewers. And since ras al hanout can be hard to find, we went with a blend of cumin, coriander and black pepper. A bit of smoked paprika added the requisite Basque touch. We finished with a drizzle of honey, which heightened the flavor of the pork and seasonings.

Don't cut the tenderloin too small. Cutting it into 1- to 1½-inch pieces produced more surface area, allowing the spice rub to quickly penetrate and season the meat. Any smaller and the meat cooked too quickly.

1. In a medium bowl, combine the coriander, cumin, paprika, salt and pepper. Add the pork and toss to coat evenly, massaging the spices into the meat until no dry rub remains. Let the pork sit at room temperature for at least 30 minutes and up to 1 hour. Meanwhile, in another bowl, combine the lemon juice, honey and garlic. Set aside.

2. In a large skillet over high, heat 1 tablespoon of the oil until barely smoking. Add the meat in a single layer and cook without moving until deeply browned on one side, about 3 minutes. Using tongs, flip the pork and cook, turning occasionally, until cooked through and browned all over, another 2 to 3 minutes. Off the heat, pour the lemon juice-garlic mixture over the meat and toss to evenly coat, then transfer to a serving platter. Sprinkle the oregano over the pork and drizzle with the remaining 1 tablespoon of oil. Serve with lemon wedges.

Chicken Teriyaki Rice Bowls
(*Teriyaki Donburi*)

Start to finish: **40 minutes** / Servings: **4**

4 tablespoons sake, divided

4 tablespoons plus 1 teaspoon soy sauce, divided

1½ pounds boneless, skinless chicken thighs, trimmed and cut into 1-inch pieces

¼ cup mirin

2 teaspoons white sugar

1 tablespoon finely grated fresh ginger

1½ cups finely shredded green cabbage

3 medium scallions, thinly sliced on diagonal

2 teaspoons unseasoned rice vinegar

¼ teaspoon toasted sesame oil

2 tablespoons cornstarch

4 teaspoons grapeseed or other neutral oil, divided

3 cups cooked Japanese-style short-grain rice, hot

Contrary to popular belief, "teriyaki" refers not to a sauce, but a technique. Meat is seared, broiled or grilled then lacquered with a glaze of soy, mirin and sugar. In this recipe, our adaptation of one taught to us by Japanese cooking expert Elizabeth Andoh, chicken thighs are briefly marinated to become tender. A coating of cornstarch gives the pieces just a hint of crispness. "Donburi" refers to individual one-bowl meals of rice with various toppings, as well as to the deep bowls that are used for serving. To our chicken teriyaki donburi, a simple slaw adds texture and freshness, rounding out the dish beautifully.

Don't forget to drain the chicken before coating it with cornstarch. Excess liquid will cause splattering during cooking.

1. In a medium bowl, whisk together 3 tablespoons of sake and 1 teaspoon of soy sauce. Add the chicken and toss. Let stand at room temperature for 20 minutes or cover and refrigerate for up to 2 hours. Meanwhile, in a small saucepan over medium, combine the remaining 1 tablespoon sake, 3 tablespoons of the remaining soy sauce, the mirin and sugar. Cook, stirring, until the sugar is dissolved, about 1 minute. Off heat, stir in the ginger; set aside.

2. In a medium bowl, toss the cabbage and scallions with the remaining 1 tablespoon soy sauce, the rice vinegar and sesame oil. Set aside. Drain the chicken in a fine mesh strainer. Wipe out the bowl, then return the chicken to it. Sprinkle with the cornstarch and toss to coat.

3. In a 12-inch nonstick skillet over medium-high, heat 2 teaspoons of grapeseed oil until barely smoking. Add half the chicken in an even layer and cook without stirring until well browned on the bottom and the edges turn opaque, 3 to 4 minutes. Flip and cook without stirring until well browned on the second side, about another 3 minutes. Transfer to a clean bowl and repeat with the remaining 2 teaspoons oil and remaining chicken.

4. Wipe out the skillet, then return the chicken to the pan. Pour in the soy sauce–ginger mixture and stir to coat. Cook over medium-high, stirring, until the liquid is syrupy and the chicken is glazed, about 2 minutes. Remove from the heat. Divide the rice among 4 bowls. Top with the cabbage mixture and chicken.